WHAT SHALL I SAY?

A GUIDE TO LETTER-
WRITING FOR LADIES

London
JAMES BOWDEN
10 HENRIETTA STREET
COVENT GARDEN, W.C.
1898

MEMBER OF
INDEPENDENT PUBLISHERS GUILD

© 1994 PRYOR PUBLICATIONS

75 Dargate Road, Yorkletts, Whitstable,
Kent CT5 3AE, England.

Tel. & Fax: (0227) 274655

Specialist in Facsimile Reproductions.

ISBN 0 946014 26 4

A CIP Record for this book is available from the British Library.

*Pryor Publications wish to thank
Peter Stockham for his advice and assistance
in the publication of this book.*

Printed in Ireland by ColourBooks Ltd.

CONTENTS

FROM MISTRESS—

APPLICATION FOR SITUATION AS—

7

10

Forms for addressing the Royal Family, the Nobility, Church Dignitaries, Officers of State, etc., etc.

The Queen

Commence.—Madam, Most Gracious Sovereign, May it please your Majesty.

Conclude.—I have the honour to remain your Majesty's most loyal subject and obedient servant.

Envelope to be addressed.—To the Queen's Most Excellent Majesty.

Princes of the Blood Royal

Commence.—Sir (or Madam), May it please your Royal Highness.

Conclude.—I have the honour to remain, Sir (or Madam), your Royal Highness's most obedient servant.

Envelope to be addressed.—To His (or Her) Royal Highness the Prince of Wales.

Other Branches of the Royal Family

Commence.—Sir (or Madam).

Conclude.—I have the honour to remain, Sir (or Madam), your Highness's most obedient servant.

Envelope to be addressed.—To His (or Her) Highness (or Serene Highness) the Prince (or Princess) of ———

The Nobility—A Duke or Duchess

Commence.—My Lord Duke (or Madam).

Conclude.—I have the honour to remain, My Lord Duke (or Madam), your Grace's very obedient servant.

Envelope to be addressed.—To His Grace the Duke of ———, K.T., or To Her Grace the Duchess of ———

A Marquis (or Marchioness)

Commence.—My Lord Marquis (or Madam).

Conclude.—I have the honour to remain, My Lord Marquis (or Madam), your very faithful and obedient servant.

Envelope to be addressed.—To the Most Noble the Marquis (or Marchioness) of ———

An Earl or Countess

Commence.—My Lord (or Madam).

Conclude.—I have the honour to remain, My Lord, your obedient servant.

Envelope to be addressed.—To the Right Honourable the Earl (or Countess) of ———

A Viscount or Viscountess

Commence.—My Lord (or Madam).

Conclude.—I have the honour to be, My Lord (or Madam), your most obedient servant.

Envelope to be addressed.—To the Right Honourable the Viscount or the Viscountess ———

A Baron or Baroness

Commence.—My Lord (or Madam).

Conclude.—I am, My Lord (or Madam), your obedient servant.

Envelope to be addressed.—To the Right Honourable the Lord or the Lady ———

A Baronet and His Wife

Commence.—Sir (or Madam).

Conclude.—I have the honour to remain, Sir (or Madam), your obedient servant.

Letters to be addressed.—To Sir John ———, Bart., or to Lady ———

In formal and official communications Dukes and Duchesses are styled *Most* Noble, Marquises and Marchionesses *Most* Honourable, and Earls and Countesses, Viscounts and Viscountesses, Barons and Baronesses, *Right* Honourable.

The Children of the Nobility

The eldest sons of Dukes, Marquises and Earls take by courtesy their father's second title, being addressed accordingly; their wives of course assume the same rank.

Younger sons of Dukes and Marquises and eldest sons of Earls take the title of Lord. Daughters of Dukes, Marquises and Earls take the title of Lady.

The younger sons of Earls and the sons of Viscounts and Barons are styled The Honourable ————. The daughters of Dukes, Marquises and Earls are addressed as The Lady Mary ————

If a Duke's daughter marry a Peer, she assumes the rank of her husband. If she be unmarried or have married a commoner, she still remains a lady in her own right, and is styled, The Lady Mary ————

In writing to the younger sons and all the daughters of Dukes and Marquises and the daughters of Earls,

Commence.—My Lord (Madam, or if preferred, My Lady).

Conclude.—I have the honour to remain, My Lord (or Madam, or My Lady), your obedient servant.

Envelope to be addressed.—To The Lord —— or The Lady ————

In addressing younger sons of Earls and sons and daughters of Viscounts and Barons,

Commence.—Sir (or Madam).

Conclude.—I am, Sir (or Madam), your obedient servant.

Envelope to be addressed.—To the Honourable ————

The wives of Baronets are addressed as Lady —————— or whatever the husband's surname may be. Peers and their wives and the sons and daughters of Peers, and the wives of the sons of Peers, must be addressed as The Lady ————. The sons and daughters of Baronets are addressed merely as Mr, Mrs, or Miss.

Knights

Commence.—Sir.

Conclude.—I am, Sir.

The envelope to be addressed. — To Sir George ————, adding K.C.B. or any other initials to which he is entitled. The wife of a Knight is addressed as, To Lady ————, not The Lady ————

The Clergy

ARCHBISHOPS.

Commence.—My Lord Archbishop.

Conclude.—I am, My Lord Archbishop, your Grace's very obedient servant.

Envelope to be addressed.—To His Grace the Lord Archbishop of ————

BISHOPS.

Commence.—My Lord Bishop.

Conclude.—I am, My Lord, your obedient servant.

Envelope to be addressed.—To the Right Rev. the Lord Bishop of ————

DEANS.

Commence.—Reverend Sir, or Mr Dean.

Conclude accordingly.—I am, Reverend Sir, or Mr Dean.

Envelope to be addressed.—To the Very Rev. the Dean of ————, adding any academic degrees to which he may be entitled.

ARCHDEACONS.

Commence.—Reverend Sir, or Mr Archdeacon, and *conclude* in the same way.

Envelope to be addressed.—To the Venerable Archdeacon ————

When writing to ordinary Clergymen,

Commence. — Sir, or Reverend Sir, and *conclude* in the same way.

The envelope to be addressed.—To the Rev. John ————, adding M.A. or any other aca-

14

demic degrees to which he is entitled. If he hold a Doctor's degree he may be addressed as the Rev. Dr ———

Note that the wives of Archbishops, Bishops, and other Church dignitaries are addressed by their husband's surname, as Mrs Temple, Mrs Creighton, etc.

Ambassadors, Plenipotentiaries, and Foreign Governors have the title of Excellency added to their ordinary rank.

Commence.—Your Excellency.

Conclude.—I am, My Lord, or, I am, Sir, (according to the rank of the person addressed), your Excellency's obedient servant.

Envelope to be addressed.—To His Excellency the Marquis of ———

Consuls

Commence and *conclude* according to rank.

The envelope to be addressed.—To ———, Consul to Her Britannic Majesty at ———

Judges, etc.

Judges who are Privy Councillors are entitled to be addressed as Right Honourable; those who are not Privy Councillors are addressed as Honourable.

The Lord Chancellor

Commence and *conclude*, as a Peer, according to rank.

Envelope to be addressed.—To the Right Honourable The Lord High Chancellor.

The Lord Chief Justice

Commence and *conclude* with My Lord.

Envelope to be addressed.—To the Right Honourable ———, according to rank.

The Lord Advocate

Commence and *conclude.*—My Lord.

Envelope to be addressed.—To the Right Honourable the Lord Advocate.

Master of the Rolls

Commence and *conclude*, as to a Judge.

Envelope to be addressed.—The Right Honourable the Master of the Rolls.

Puisne Judges

Commence and *conclude.*—Sir.

Envelope to be addressed. — To Mr Justice ———

Army and Navy

In the Army and Navy, the person addressed is styled according to his rank, the post he holds being also stated thus, To Admiral the Lord ———, K.C.B., To Field-Marshal the Earl of ———, V.C., To Major the Honourable ———, To Captain Arthur ———, R.N., etc.

Barristers

Barristers are styled Esquire, thus: To Arthur ———, Esquire, Q.C., M.P.

Medical Men

Medical and Professional Men generally are styled Esquire. If the person addressed holds the M.D. degree he may be addressed as A. ——— Esq., M.D., or as Dr ——— It is best, however, when writing to Medical Men to fall in with the form most in use in connection with the person addressed, as some Medical Men who do not hold the M.D. dislike being addressed as Doctor, while on the other hand others who do not hold it invariably speak of and style themselves as Doctor ———.

Rules for Letter-writing.

NOTEPAPER

THE notepaper should always be clean. A woman who uses soiled notepaper must not complain if her correspondent suspect her of being slovenly and untidy.

White notepaper is always correct. Those who prefer paper in fancy colours should see to it that the colouring is not so dark as to render the handwriting difficult to read.

Don't use very common paper unless compelled. Stationery is so very cheap now, that there is very little excuse for writing letters on paper that is apt to run or to show through on the other side.

INK

Black ink is always 'good form.' Those who prefer violet or fancy ink must at least consider their correspondents sufficiently to avoid inks which are so faint as to make the handwriting difficult to read.

DATE AND ADDRESS

Always write the full address and date distinctly in the right hand corner. The habit of heading letters 'London, Saturday,' or 'Paris, Sunday,' is reprehensible, as it is possible that your correspondent may have forgotten the address. And should he chance to be absent, the Post-Office authorities have then no address

to which to return your letter. If your correspondence is considerable, you will find it convenient to have the address stamped on your notepaper. For business people the address may be printed, but for private correspondence it is more usual to have the address stamped with a 'die.' Any stationer would get a 'die' cut for you at a cost of a few shillings. But if you prefer, as many persons do, to write the address, let it be very legible, and be careful that numbers are especially so, as a mistake in a number may give yourself and your correspondent much trouble and cause irritating delays. The date, which should never be omitted, is generally written in the right-hand corner immediately under the address. Some ladies prefer to write the address at the bottom of the letter in the left-hand corner, but it is best to put it at the top in the right-hand corner, when you commence the letter. Then there will be no possibility of its being omitted.

PUNCTUATION.

Every one should acquire some knowledge of the Rules of Punctuation, and should make use of that knowledge when writing letters, whether business or private. The omission of a punctuation mark may give quite another meaning than intended to a sentence. The end of a sentence should always be marked by a full stop (.), and by the use of a capital letter when beginning the next sentence. To put a dash (—) instead of a full stop, as is sometimes seen, is incorrect, although it is less objectionable than the habit some offenders have of beginning new sentences with a small letter. The dash has its own place in punctuation, and its use should be restricted accordingly. Notes of exclamation (!) are not often used in letter-writing unless to emphasise some point strongly; but when a question is asked, the note of interrogation (?) should be placed at the end of the question. Inverted commas (" ") are used for quotation.

SALUTATION

Begin the salutation on the left-hand side of the paper, leaving a little space between it and the address and date. In writing to strangers in a formal way commence 'Sir' or 'Madam.' If you do not wish to be too formal, commence 'Dear Sir' or 'Dear Madam.' Correspondents whom you know personally should be addressed as 'Dear Mr Brown' or 'Dear Mrs Smith.' If you are very intimate you may say, 'My dear Mr Brown' or 'My dear Mrs Smith.' Friends whom in personal intercourse you call by their Christian name should of course be addressed in the same way in letters, either as 'Dear Mary,' 'My dear Mary,' or 'Dearest Mary,' according to the closeness of the intimacy.

In writing to strangers or to those whom you do not know well, it is customary to add your correspondent's name at the close of the letter, though some persons prefer to place the name before the salutation. Appended are two letters illustrating this. The first example given is the most usual.

> *Ivy Lodge,*
> *Victoria Road,*
> *Balham, S.W.,*
> *January 1st, 1898.*

Dear Madam,

      In reply to your letter asking me to fix a date on which I could see you respecting the matter that you wish to discuss with me, I shall be at home next Monday afternoon, and shall be pleased to see you if that date is convenient. If it should be inconvenient to you, perhaps you will let me know, and I would arrange to be at home and disengaged on another afternoon.

> Yours faithfully,
>
> Rose Mason.

Mrs Sidney Harper.

Ivy Lodge,
Victoria Road,
Balham, S.W.,
Jan. 2nd, 1898.

To Arthur Williams, Esq.

Dear Sir,

I have received your note asking me to fix a date upon which you could call to discuss the proposed testimonial to our Rector, Mr Greene. Would Monday afternoon at three o'clock suit you? If so, I should be pleased to see you then.

Yours sincerely,

Rose Mason.

Many persons prefer, when communicating with entire strangers or correspondents with whom they wish to maintain entirely formal relations, to adopt the third person, thus :

The Croft,
Moorlands,
Jan. 4th, 1898.

Mrs Armitage-Browne has to thank Mrs King for her communication, but regrets that she does not see her way to allow her daughter to take any part in the theatrical performance referred to. She therefore returns, with her thanks and compliments, the papers which Mrs King has been good enough to send.

If this more ceremonious form be adopted, the writer must be careful to word the letter so clearly that the pronouns do not become confused. Here, for instance is a communication in which it is by no means easy to say to whom the numerous 'hers' and 'shes' refer.

Mrs Compton Brown's daughter has told her
20

of her accidental meeting with Mrs Smith and of the invitation she has been good enough to give, but she regrets to say that she is not disengaged on the evening in question.

For general purposes, the plain ' Madam ' or ' Dear Madam ' answers the purpose equally well and is certainly simpler. But it must be remembered that to address a correspondent to whom you are known personally as ' Madam ' or ' Sir ' would generally be understood as a ' snub,' or at all events as intimating that the writer of the letter wished to maintain only formal relations with the person addressed. In fact, to address any one of your own social position, to whom you are known personally, as ' Dear Sir ' or ' Dear Madam,' instead of ' Dear Mr Smith ' or ' Dear Mrs Robinson,' would in all probability be taken as indicating a certain ' stand-offishness ' on the part of the writer in regard to the person addressed.

A word against undue familiarity to any one but a very intimate friend or a relation may not be out of place. Well-bred persons object to being addressed in a too familiar or ' gushing ' way. If they wish to cultivate your acquaintance, the fact will soon be evident from the tone of their letters to you. Then, but not till then, you may respond, if you wish to, with proportionate friendliness. It is always possible to write pleasantly and even cordially, without lapsing into effusiveness ; but remember that if your correspondent be older than yourself, or of a superior social position, you will do well to let the advances come, in the first place, from her or from him, as the case may be, not from you.

Now in regard to the point whether men correspondents be styled ' Esquire ' or ' Mr.' The usage of ' Esquire ' was originally rather limited. It is now used much more generally. In writing to a tradesman at his trade address, you would address him as ' Mr Brown,' but merchants and business men generally (especially when letters are addressed to their private

residences), are very commonly styled 'Esquire.'
A few old-fashioned folk still limit the use of
'Esquire' to the professional classes and gentlemen of independent means (and there is much
to be said in support of the word being so
limited), but nowadays when successful trades-
men are often entitled to write J.P. after their
names, the title of 'Esquire' is used with very
little restriction. In writing to a stranger of
whose social position you are not sure, it is
always safer to address him as 'Esquire.'
Very few persons resent being so addressed,
even if they know they are entitled only to
plain 'Mr.' But a good many who think themselves eligible for the more distinctive title
would resent to be dubbed 'Mr.'

Now we come to

THE LETTER.

First, a word in regard to the handwriting,
which cannot be too plain. Legibility is the
first requisite. Never mind about flourishes
or 'style.' If your handwriting is pleasant to
look at as well as easy to read, so much the
better ; but never sacrifice legibility to
show.

No one admires a 'style' which is difficult
to read, and if you hanker to be 'admired,' as
vain persons all do, you would, for your own
sake, do well to choose some other field in which
to 'show off' than in affecting an eccentric
handwriting.

Your letters will never be altogether welcome
—even to those who love you—if to read them
is a trial alike to the eyes and to the temper.
It is not given to every one to write prettily,
but if your handwriting be naturally bad, the
necessity for making it clear is all the more
imperative. To write an illegible letter—unless
you are absolutely incapable of writing clearly
—is to act inconsiderately and discourte-
ously.

If your letter be a business communication,

word it as definitely, as simply, and as shortly as possible. Figures should be carefully formed, and in letters of importance it is a good plan to give the figures in two ways, thus—'Five hundred pounds (£500)'—to prevent any possible misunderstanding.

One of the greatest arts in letter-writing is that of saying in the fewest words what one has to say without appearing abrupt. In writing a letter the person to whom it is addressed should always be borne in mind, for the type of letter that would be pleasing to one person might be distinctly distasteful to another.

For ordinary letters the conversational style is pleasantest. One hears the remark, 'So-and-So writes so exactly as he talks, it is like having a chat with him.'

But for business letters the main subject should be introduced at once, and clearly, and with as much brevity as is compatible with courtesy.

Another point in which the individuality of a writer of letters comes out is its methods of *beginning* and *ending*. Stereotyped forms should always, if possible, be avoided. Such as, 'Just a few lines to say;' or endings such as, 'In greatest haste,' and other types too well known, alas! to need quoting.

Avoid underlining as much as possible. This is a bad habit, which belongs to women rather than men.

LETTERS FOR LADIES

INVITATIONS AND REPLIES

Dinner Invitation

Mr and Mrs B. request the pleasure of Mrs Z.'s company at dinner on Tuesday, November the 20th, at 7.30.

18 *Avenue Road*, 10*th Nov.*

Reply—Accepting

Mrs Z. has much pleasure in accepting Mr and Mrs B.'s kind invitation to dinner on the 20th of November.

6 *Holland Park*, 11*th Nov.*

Reply—Declining

Mrs Z. regrets that a prior engagement (or any other proper excuse may be inserted) prevents her having the pleasure of accepting Mr and Mrs B.'s kind invitation for 20th November.

6 *Holland Park*, 11*th Nov.*

If the Invitation is from an intimate friend the following form would do.

Dear Mrs ——,

Will you and your husband give us the pleasure of your company at dinner on Monday, 1st Jan., at 8 o'clock ?

With kind regards,

Believe me,

Yours sincerely,

AMY S.

3 *Rutland Gardens, 26th Dec.*

Reply—Accepting

Dear Mrs S.,

My husband and I will have much pleasure in accepting your kind invitation for 1st Jan.

With kind regards,

Yours sincerely,

ROSE D.

1 *Cleveland Place, 27th Dec.*

Reply—Declining

Dear Mrs S.,

My husband and I much regret that a prior engagement prevents our accepting your kind invitation for 1st Jan. I hope your little dinner will be as great a success as usual.

Yours sincerely,

ROSE D.

Cleveland Place, 27th Dec.

Invitation to a Musical Evening

7 Montrose Place,
1st Oct. 18—

Dear Mrs ——,

On Wednesday, Oct. 10, I am giving another of my musical evenings. I do hope you and Mr —— will come, and bring Florence and Mary. Their playing is so much admired. I do envy you those girls!

One thing will delight you. I have managed to engage that marvellous child-violinist. He is to play two solos, and also in two quartets.

With best regards,

Yours very truly,

MARION ——.

Reply—Accepting

8 Avenue Road,
4th Oct. 18—

Dear Mrs ——,

Your musical evenings are so delightful, I could not think of missing one if I could possibly help it. My husband regrets that he is unable to accompany me, and begs me to make his apologies for him, as he has been called away suddenly to see an old army friend who is ill. However, I will bring Florence and Mary.

Thank you for the kind things you say of them.

Yours most sincerely,
HELEN ——.

Reply—Declining

8 Avenue Road,
2nd Oct. 18—

Dear Mrs ——,

You know what an attraction your musical evenings have for me, for I am rarely absent; but, unluckily, I must forego what would have been a great pleasure, for my husband and I have promised to be present at an entertainment in aid of a charity. So many thanks all the same.

Yours most sincerely,
HELEN ——.

**An informal
Invitation to an
Evening Gathering**

Ashton,
1st Nov. 18—

Dear Mrs C.,

We are anxious for a few of our friends to come in after dinner on Thursday evening to meet our son, who is home

from America. Will you and Mr C.
and your daughters join us? It would
add much to our pleasure to have you
all with us. If your son has returned
from Paris I need hardly say how glad
we should be to see him too. We
propose to wind up the evening with a
dance.

With kindest regards,
Yours sincerely,
MAUD H.

Reply—Accepting

Hartover,
2nd Nov. 18—

Dear Mrs H.,

It will give us all much pleasure
to join you on Thursday evening. We
look forward with interest to renewing
our acquaintance with your son, whom
we remember as an exceptionally bright
and (I may say it to his mother) hand-
some boy.

With kindest regards,
Yours truly,
MARY C.

Reply—Declining

Hartover,
2nd Nov. 18—

Dear Mrs H.,

It is with real regret that I
find myself obliged to decline so kind
and friendly an invitation as yours. But
we leave for Scotland to-morrow.

Will you remember us cordially to
your son, whom I remember very well?

With kindest regards,
Yours truly,
MARY C.

**Invitation to
a Picnic**

Wood Grange,
1st Aug. 18—

Dear Mrs ——,

The weather is so inviting and our woods look so cool and lovely, that we propose to make up a gipsy party and camp out for the day on Thursday next. Our girls are home from school, and we have a small army of their school-fellows domiciled at present under our roof. My brother from India is here, too, with his wife. We were wondering if you and your young folks would care to join us? If so, would you be at Wood Grange not later than 10 o'clock? and *please* let the girls wear suitable dresses, for we have made up our minds not to be afraid of hedges or ditches or of a chance shower, which so often, alas! baptises a picnic party!

Hoping you will not disappoint us,

Yours sincerely,
ALICE ——.

Reply—Accepting

Endleigh,
2nd Aug. 18—

Dear Mrs ——,

Of all things my youngsters love a picnic, and I must confess that we older folks fully enter into their feelings, so we shall accept your kind invitation with much pleasure.

Yours it seems is to be a *real* picnic, and not a sort of rural garden-party got up to show off pretty dresses and carry on flirtations. That sort of picnic is not at all to my liking. Harry is going to bring his banjo, so we may get up a little dance if you like.

With kindest regards,

Yours sincerely,
MARY ——.

Reply—Declining

Endleigh,
2nd Aug. 18—

Dear Mrs ——,

I am much disappointed to have to decline so enticing an invitation, but on Thursday next my husband's two old maiden aunts are going to bear down on us, and, as you know, they always expect the whole family at home to receive them, and would never forgive the absence of even one of the children.

My young folks are exceedingly doleful. Harry in particular, who has been venting his feelings characteristically by playing the lowest note in the bass on the piano at minute intervals, like a funeral bell.

Well, I hope you will have a good time.

Yours sincerely,
MARY ——.

Afternoon 'At Home' Invitation Card (Formal)

Mr and Mrs Benson.

Mrs Harold Hurst

At Home

Saturday, 3rd Jan.
From 4 o'clock.   Music.
Tower House.   *R.S.V.P.*

Same—Informal

Tower House,
13th Dec. 18—

Dear Mrs Benson,

I shall be 'At Home' on Saturday, 3rd Jan., from 4 o'clock. Can you and your husband find time to come?

I expect some exceptionally nice people.

Yours faithfully,
HONOR HURST.

Reply—Accepting (Formal)

Mr and Mrs Benson have pleasure in accepting Mrs Harold Hurst's kind invitation for 3rd Jan.

Merton House,
    16th Dec. 18—

Reply—Accepting (Informal)

Merton House,
    16th Dec. 18—

Dear Mrs Hurst,

My husband and myself will be most happy to accept your kind invitation for 3rd Jan.

Is it too early to send all good Xmas wishes?

Yours truly,
BERTHA BENSON.

Reply—Declining (Formal)

Mr and Mrs Benson regret that a previous engagement prevents their accepting Mrs Harold Hurst's kind invitation for 3rd Jan.

Merton House,
    16th Dec. 18—

Reply—Declining (Informal)

Merton House,
    16th Dec. 18—

Dear Mrs Hurst,

Unfortunately my husband and myself have an engagement on 3rd Jan., otherwise it would have given us much pleasure to accept your kind invitation.

With cordial regards,
Yours truly,
BERTHA BENSON.

**Letter inviting
a friend to
pay a visit**
The Grange, Nailsea,
    6th Aug. 18—

My dear Etta,

Do take pity on my loneliness and come and spend a few weeks with

me. Our grounds are now perfection, and I can promise you some good boating and picnics, for which you used to have a weakness.

Don't say it is impossible, for it is so long since we met; and now everyone is from home we could get a nice time all to ourselves.

Looking eagerly for a reply.

Yours affectionately,
                    DORA MICHELSON.

Reply—Accepting

The Hollies, Dulwich,
18th Aug. 18—

My dear Dora,

Nothing can give me more pleasure than to accept your invitation, so on Monday next, if convenient to you, you may expect

Your friend,
ETTA.

Reply—Declining

The Hollies, Dulwich,
18th Aug. 18—

My dear Dora,

I am so sorry and so disappointed, but it is quite impossible for me to leave home just now. My mother, whose health has been failing for some time, is now seriously ill, so I could not think of leaving her. So you will understand.

Yours affectionately,
ETTA.

Invitation to
a Funeral

Mrs —— begs to inform Mr —— that the funeral of the late Mr —— will take place at Highgate Cemetery on the 20th inst. at 4 o'clock.

Reply

Mr —— thanks Mrs —— for her letter informing him of the date of Mr ——'s funeral. He will certainly not fail to pay a last tribute of respect by being present.

Invitation to a Christening

Mrs —— requests the pleasure of the company of Mr and Mrs —— on the occasion of the christening of her little son.

The ceremony will take place at the Parish Church, on Tuesday, the 9th inst., at 11.30.

Reception from
4 — 7   *R. S. V. P.*

(This means, Réspondez s'il vous plait—reply if you please.)

Handsworth House,
   Weston, 2nd May 18—

Reply

Mr and Mrs —— will have much pleasure in being present at the christening of the little son and heir, on the 9th.

Melrose Park,
   3rd May 18—

Same—Informal

Handsworth House,
Weston, 2nd May 18—

Dear Mrs ——,

Will you and your husband do us the pleasure of being present at the christening of our son, on the 9th? It will take place at the Parish Church, at 11.30.

There will be a reception in the afternoon, from 4—7.

Sincerely yours,
BEATRICE MONSON.

Reply—Informal   *Melrose Park,*
                        3rd May 18—

Dear Mrs Monson,

    We shall have much pleasure in being present at the christening of your little son, and will call upon you in the afternoon.

           Yours very truly,
              CAROLINE ———.

**Invitation for children
of a friend to
Juvenile Party**   *St Vincent House,*
                      24th Nov. 18—

Dear Mrs Percival,

    Would you allow all your young folks to join in our festivities on 5th Dec. ? It is our small Eva's birthday, and we expect quite a large gathering. If your children can come, will you kindly send them by 4 o'clock, as so many of the children are so young that they must leave not later than 9 o'clock. Hoping for a favourable reply,

           Yours faithfully,
              LENA RIVERS.

Reply—Accepting   *Melrose,*
                         25th Nov. 18—

Dear Mrs Rivers,

    My children are delighted to think of joining Eva's party of young friends on 5th Dec. But there are so many of them that I fear they will materially swell your numbers !

    With kind regards,

           Yours,
             ROSE PERCIVAL.

Reply—Declining   *Melrose,*
                         25th Nov. 18—

Dear Mrs Rivers,

    When you hear that baby has measles, I am sure you will see

in it sufficient reason for my keeping her brothers and sisters away from other children for some time to come.

I have not told any one of them, or we should have floods of tears.

Always yours,

ROSE PERCIVAL.

Wedding Invitation

Holmwood,
1st July 18—

My dear Maud,

We have fixed Tuesday the 18th as the date of Mabel's marriage. We were in hopes we might keep her with us until the Spring, but her future husband leaves for India sooner than he expected, so we are reluctantly obliged to hurry on the ceremony. You, as my oldest friend, will, I know, sympathise with me on what is a sad occasion to a mother at any time, but to me more especially sad, because my only child will be so far separated from me, and for so many years! Still we must make the day one of rejoicing to others, so will you come and help me? Your presence always seems to make things go better.

Your affectionate friend,

MARGARET BURNS.

Reply—Accepting

Arneleigh,
2nd July 18—

My dear Margaret,

Your news comes quite as a surprise to me. You seemed so sure of keeping Mabel until the Spring. But after all, if a parting must come, it cannot matter much that it should be a few months sooner. In fact, it gives you less time to think sad thoughts, and the

necessary hurry and bustle will help to carry you through.

Of course I will come and do all I can to assist you.

Your affectionate friend,
MAUD.

Reply—Declining *Arneleigh,*
2nd July 18—

My dear Margaret,

How sorry I am both for your sake and for mine that the 18th is the date fixed upon for Mabel's marriage. You must know how gladly I would have been with you on this particular day, for I have scarcely been absent from any important event in your life since we were at school together, but as fate will have it, Tom and I start for America on the 10th. Had we known sooner we might have so arranged our affairs as to remain in England until after the 18th. Now I fear it is impossible.

You must not allow yourself to get depressed about Mabel. You are not losing her when you give her to a good husband, and the time will soon pass, and you will have her home again. I will write Mabel.

Your affectionate friend,
MAUD.

Letter from a governess to her mother saying she is unhappy in her situation *Belview Lodge,*
16th Oct. 18—

My dear Mother,

I do not really think I can remain in this situation. I have been here for a month, and I have never had a sympathetic word from Mrs Ellis, who treats me exactly like a machine

36

I am expected to do much of the work which ought to belong to the nursemaid, so when my charges are in bed, instead of having a little time to myself for reading or music or mending my clothes, I am expected to see to the wardrobes of all the children, put the schoolroom in order for the next day, and go and sit with the baby if it wakes up, which it does nearly every night. I must of necessity sit with no other light than that of a shaded night-light! So it is impossible to read or do any needlework. This is very dreary, as you may imagine, more especially as I can hear singing and music and sometimes dancing going on in the drawing-room.

Ada and Maud Ellis are about my own age, but they never come and chat with me, taking their cue from their mother, no doubt.

They live a life which is one round of gaiety, and I do feel the contrast so painfully. Why should some girls have everything and others nothing?

I have my meals in the schoolroom with my two elder pupils, and I never go out except when I take these children for their walk.

How I think of the bright fireside at home, and of you and father and the girls! and how I wish myself back!

Surely all situations are not as trying as this one. Tell me if I must inform Mrs Ellis I wish to leave.

With best love to all of you,
Your loving daughter,
AMY.

The mother's reply

Elm Cottage,
17th Oct. 18—

My dearest Child,

Your letter is a great grief to us all. We never dreamed you were not

happy, as your letters (for our sakes, no doubt) have all been so bright, cheerful and uncomplaining until this last one.

Undoubtedly, it should be no part of your duty to sit with the baby in the evenings. If it is the duty of any one, it is distinctly that of the nursemaid, and not of the governess.

I think I would speak to Mrs Ellis about this matter—you could do it nicely, you know—and remind her that you were promised your evenings to yourself.

If you get your evenings to read and amuse yourself, or to study, I think you would find yourself much happier.

As for the unsympathetic attitude of the grown-up part of the family, I would think as little as I could about it, and try to gain the affection of your pupils. Their mother and elder sisters appear to be too fond of their own pleasures to take much interest in the children, so they will be naturally particularly open to kindness such as you could show them. If you do this the whole atmosphere will change for you.

Wherever you go you will find some hard things and some unpleasant ones, so if I were you I would not give up after one month, but try a little longer, and see if things don't improve.

One lesson is open to you to learn—one of the most important of all to a woman —patient, cheerful endurance. This lesson once learnt will carry you further than most things in life.

Do not think I do not sympathise. I only want my dear girl not to turn her back on a difficulty, but to face it bravely, so as to strengthen character.

Of course, if after you have tried a time longer you find the place thoroughly

uncongenial to you, you must leave it, for nothing is worse than being a square thing in a round hole.

We all send you our dear love.

MOTHER.

Birthday letter—To a mother from her daughter at school

Dansbury College,
11th June 18—

My dearest Mother,

How can I express my joy at having you still with us to congratulate on another birthday ? It seems specially nice this year, because your illness made us all so sad, and the contrast of having you well again is so great.

My dear mother, I will try more than ever to be a comfort to you, not only by working well at my studies, but by being all you can wish in every respect.

I am trying to cultivate tidy habits, and have the reputation here of being much improved. But you must judge when I come home for the holidays.

The antimacassar I send is my own work.

With much love to dear father and little Willie, and an extra portion for yourself, as it is your birthday,

Believe me,
Your loving daughter,
RACHEL.

Another, from a daughter to her father who is from home

Millwood,
1st Feb. 18—

My dearest Father,

How we all wish you were at home to receive our birthday wishes in person !

Well, we must make letters a bad substitute, I suppose.

39

Though away from us we all hope you will have a very happy birthday, and you may be sure we shall be thinking of you most lovingly.

Your particular chair by the fireside looks very empty without you.

Do come home as soon as possible to mother and

Your affectionate daughter,
EVA.

From a sister to her young brother   *Tide Walk,*
Worthing, 2nd Aug. 18—

My dear Jack,

The peace and quiet of our establishment is wonderful since your departure. Also, Jane says the house keeps tidy almost by itself since Master John has gone! Yet we do miss you most dreadfully, and would willingly put up with some noise and untidiness to have you still with us.

I have kept your numerous pets in order as far as possible. But one catastrophe I was unable to avert,—your favourite grey cat made a breakfast of your white mice!

When next you come home you will find something that will delight you. Father is having a little shed put up for you to do your carpentry in!

At first I thought I would not tell you about it, but let you find it as a pleasant surprise, but on second thoughts I could not deny you the pleasure of thinking about it beforehand. Mother is writing to you herself, so I will leave her to tell her own news.

Willie and Teddie are out in their goat-carriage. With much love,

Your affectionate sister,
EMMA.

**Letter from a servant
to her mother**

Albert Lodge,
1st June 18—

My dear Mother,

You will be pleased to hear that I reached my situation quite safely. Though I feel a little. strange at first, I think I shall like the place. There seems a good deal of work to be done, but you know I was never one to mind work if I were comfortable and kindly treated. And my mistress is very kind and pleasant. There are two dear little children here, and I am glad, as having been at home so long I should have missed the children.

My fellow-servant is very nice, and shows me where things are, and explains anything I don't understand. She made me some nice tea when I arrived last night, and would not let me do anything to help her, as she said I must be tired after my long journey.

Tell Maggie and Jim I shall send them each something when I get my first wages.

Hoping you and father and the children are well, and with best love,

I am,

Your dutiful daughter,

MARY JENKINS.

**Birthday letter
to a sister**

Brixton,
30th July 18—

My dear Mabel,

So you will really be of age to-morrow!

Don't I remember my twenty-first birthday! yet it does seem a long time ago—five years ago! and here am I married, with a little son who has commenced to celebrate what he calls 'berf-days.'

Well, dear, that your birthday may be very happy is the wish of

Your loving sister,

NORAH.

Birthday letter to a brother

Weston,
12th July 18—

My dear Percy,

Very many happy returns of the day.

We all hope you will have what you term a 'fine old time,' and we don't doubt that you will in such good company, and in that wonderful Switzerland, which, not so lucky as you, I have as yet only seen in dreams.

But for our letters, I daresay you would forget all about your birthday among such new and delightful experiences, but we at home shall not forget it, for it will be a small excitement in this 'go-to-sleep' sort of place, where we watch our shadows turn at our feet.

You won't want to be bothered by a lengthy epistle, I know, and there is really nothing to tell.

So with much love,

I remain,

Your affectionate sister,

GEORGINA.

From a schoolgirl to her mother complaining that her allowance is insufficient

Ladies' College,
Bridge North, 4th May 18—

Dearest Mother,

I am writing to beg you to increase my allowance a little, as I find it insufficient. I enclose a table of my expenditure, so that you and dear father can see exactly how I have spent my

money, also a list of things all the girls are expected to get themselves, so that you may see clearly my position. I am so sorry to trouble you, but I am quite sure you will realise that it is not extravagance on my part that causes me to ask for a little more money.

With fondest love to each and all,
Believe me,
Your loving daughter,
AMELIA.

From a daughter at school asking permission to bring home a school-friend for the holidays

Leslie House School,
Rugely, 20th July 18—

My very dear Mother,
You know how much I talked of my friend Milly Brown when last I saw you; well, her parents are going to remove to a distance during the holidays, and she says everything will be in an upset. Oh, please can't she spend her holiday with me? I should enjoy having her so much. I have not told her I am going to ask you, because she would be so disappointed if you found you could not have her. She is such a nice girl, and I am sure you would like her.

With much love,
Your affectionate daughter,
ELSIE.

Reply

Fleetwood,
13th July 18—

My dearest Elsie,
I shall be very pleased for you to bring your friend Milly Brown home with you for the holidays if her mother will allow her to come. You can tell her

43

from me that I am writing to-day to Mrs
Brown to ask if she will let her daughter
come.

Your loving mother,
MERCIE BATESON.

From a daughter at
school asking her
mother for more
pocket-money

Beinsley School for Girls,
Brighton, 19th April 18—

Dearest Mother,

This is not my day for writing to
you, but as all my pocket-money is spent,
I thought I would write and let you know
I have seen a new kind of purse and
several other things I should much like
to buy.

The weather is beautiful now, and we get
some splendid long walks. These walks
make me wish I had taken your advice
and not had such narrow-pointed shoes,
for they tire my feet.

We have commenced our out-door
sketching class already. I like it very
much.

The dinner-bell is ringing, so I must
stop.— With love to dear father and
yourself,

Your loving daughter,
ADA.

To a daughter at
school advising her
to be economical
Park Lodge,
1st May 18—

My dear Ada,

I was really surprised by your
request for more pocket-money after
your father's most liberal gift to you
when you went back to school.

What do you spend your money in,
dear? You are well supplied with all

44

necessaries, so I can only infer that you have really wasted your money. Now, my dear child, I don't want to scold or make you unhappy, but I do want to impress upon you the necessity of cultivating habits of economy. Aimless and haphazard spending will bring disaster in its wake however wealthy one may be, and the habits you form now will make or mar your future. Do not imagine that years of discretion will necessarily bring habits of discretion with them. It is what you make *yourself* that will make your future. The formation of habits is a slow process, and one in which you cannot, as in some things, make up for lost time.

I enclose five shillings, and you must write down all you spend, and send me the account when the money is gone, then I will advise you on the subject.

With much love,
Your affectionate mother,
MATILDA MERTON.

To a daughter at school inquiring about her health
2 *Dark Street*,
Maidstone, 2nd May 18—

My very dear Ella,
In your last two letters you do not mention your health, and I am a little anxious. Has your cough left you quite? And has your appetite improved? I hope you take your medicine regularly.

One thing I must impress upon you, do not on any account change your warm clothing for thinner ones, because it is warm and fine. You know that was the cause of your getting such a bad cough last spring.

With love from all,
Your devoted mother,
MARIAN MORRIS.

From a daughter at school complaining of overwork

Langham College,
3rd May 18—

My dear Parents,

I hope you will not think I have grown to dislike study, when I ask you to write to our headmistress relative to the amount of work I am given to do at present. I assure you that far from wishing to shirk my studies, I am most anxious to make the best use of my time and opportunity. I find that I cannot cover the ground required of me, even with the greatest effort. I know if I had less given me to learn I should retain it, while as things exist at present, the knowledge with which I laboriously cram my head one day is gone the next.

I spoke to the headmistress about this, but she was of opinion that the work was in no way excessive. So I am writing to you. I feel sure you will understand and help me.

With love to you both and to my dear little sister,

I am,

Your loving daughter,
MARIE.

Letter to an aunt

Leecroft,
7th Jan. 18—

My dear Aunt,

Outside the snow lies deep, and a bitter east wind is blowing, so I shall forego my usual walk and spend the time pleasantly in writing to you.

I expect you are busy looking after your poor people. What would they do without you, I wonder?

You live so much for others that when I think of you and your own beautiful life, my own seems poor and paltry.

You give up your own comforts and pleasures so cheerfully.

Well, for once, my meditations have led to something practical. I have knitted a dozen little woollen petticoats for you to distribute among the poor little mites who are so near your kind heart. The parcel is already speeding on its way to you.

Mother keeps very well, and father is robust and cheerful, as is his wont. Herbert will remain away from school this term as his chest continues delicate, but our curate is coming in for an hour a day to teach him, so he won't lose so much time as he would otherwise. He (Herbert) is much delighted at this moment with a set of fretwork tools which father brought home for him.

Already he has in imagination filled every vacant space on our walls with wonderful brackets, and I am promised a glove-box which he says I can line with red silk, though it is by no means clear to me how I can sew the same to wood. But, of course, I express myself charmed.

You will let me know when you receive the parcel, won't you?

Everyone sends love to you, and please accept a double portion from

Your affectionate niece,

ADA.

Letter to an uncle

Mill Vale,
8th Jan. 18—

My dear Uncle,

We were all most delighted to receive your letter, and to learn from it that you are so well and prospering.

We all keep well at home, but mother feels the cold very much, and occupies her warm corner in the drawing-room

all day, amusing herself with her beloved knitting and Mudie's parcel of books, which has opportunely arrived. We are having a lively time, I can tell you, owing to the roads being impassable (or nearly so) from snow-drifts.

Each morning there is an interesting and exciting discussion as to the chances of the arrival of the tradesman with our provisions. If this weather lasts we shall be reduced to tinned edibles, to which none of us are partial.

This morning the butcher came with an agonising appeal that we would order all we wanted for a week, adding encouragingly that it would keep for ever in this Arctic climate.

We have already set up a sledge, and a toboggan is in preparation. The snow makes skating an impossibility. Another treat looms ahead, in the shape of broken water-pipes. The poor birds are so starved that they come into the very house for food and shelter. We find lots of them frozen to death, though we always put out food for them.

Well, this letter must come to an end, as John has come to take it to the post, so

With love from all,

I remain,

Your affectionate niece,

NANCY.

Letter to a husband

Hazelwood,
1st March 18—

My dearest Husband,

I could not help feeling very thankful that you were safely landed on the other side of the Atlantic this morning, for March certainly came in like a lion, and a particularly angry one at that.

Our poor old mountain ash is uprooted

48

right out of the ground, and some tiles from our roof have fallen on to the conservatory roof, smashing a lot of glass and injuring the black grape vine.

If March fulfils the character with which it is credited you will have a delightful home-coming.

The house is so dull without you. It is in the evening I miss you most, when all the children are gone to bed, for as you know I always looked forward to that time as the best part of the day when you were at home, and we spent it together.

Baker has put up your new bookshelves, and they look capital, so now I long to see you congenially at work arranging your books.

All our small folks are very well. Baby is particularly brilliant and says continually, 'Want to see pappa!'

I have no more news just now, but I have a pile of small socks demanding to be mended, so with love and longing for your speedy and safe return,

Your affectionate wife,
MARGARET.

From a mother to her daughter at school *The Hawthornes,*
Whitby, 19th May 18—

My dearest Maude,

Your last letter gave me much pleasure, as it was so well written, and the sentiments you expressed were so healthy and good.

Only plod on, dear, in the path you have so wisely chosen, and you are sure to succeed.

Never let discouragement deter you from effort. It is just when one tries one's best in face of discouragement that real advancement is made.

49

D

You say it is hard that all the girls are more clever than you are. That, dear, need not trouble you. You need only do your best and leave it, the result rests with One who made some more clever than others. Moreover, your mother would much rather see you *good* than *clever*.

There is something at home for you that will simply delight you. Your father has bought you a beautiful little cream pony! Now you have something pleasant to think of till the holidays come.

Your father joins me in fondest love to you.

From your devoted mother,
MARY ELTON.

From a mother to her son at school urging him to work hard

3 *Burton St.,*
Ashley, 4th May 18—

My dearest Boy,

Your father and I were very pleased with your letter received to-day, and are quite proud of your athletic successes. But, dear, we want to hear a little more about your success in *work*. You know your last report was disappointing, for you took no distinguished place in any subject, and there was a note upon the report to the effect, that not want of *brains* but *indolence* stood in your way.

But if you make up your mind you can gladden our hearts by earning a really good report next term. Try, there's a good boy. You know you can never recall a lost opportunity, and in the future your position in life will be entirely dependent on the use you make of your present opportunities.

Your father joins me in fondest love to you.

From your loving mother,

BELINDA MASON.

To a son at school urging him to be economical

10 *Richmond Terrace, Blackheath, 4th May* 18—

My very dear Son,

We are all most gratified to hear that you are working so well and with such good results. Indeed, we are more than satisfied with you, except in one respect—you are extravagant in money matters.

The sum we give you at the beginning of each term is ample for all your requirements, yet in a few weeks you write home for more.

Now, take my advice and write down all your expenditure, and when your money is exhausted, look over your accounts, and I fancy you will see many things you could have well dispensed with.

You know extravagance is a dreadful habit to cultivate, and will inevitably bring you into difficulties when you become a man and have to face the world, whatever income you may be possessed of.

Think over what I have said, and try to act upon it, and so remove an anxiety from the mind of

Your affectionate mother,

MILLICENT JENNINGS.

To a son at school respecting a complaint of disobedience

The Oaks, Richmond, 5th May 18—

My dear Edmund,

It was with the deepest grief that I heard of your act of flagrant

disobedience this morning in a communication from Dr Ridgeworth.

You who express such a strong desire to be a brave soldier, as your dear father was, have yet to learn that in order to command you must first learn to obey.

This is the first complaint I have ever had of you, and I do sincerely hope it may be the last.

Do, my dear boy, try to redeem your character by being extra good for the remainder of the term, and so make happy

Your loving mother,

SARAH INNES.

To a son at college respecting his choice of an occupation

16 *The Crescent,*
Brixton, 6th May 18—

My dear Henry,

As this year will end your college life, I am writing to ask you if you have as yet arrived at a decision about your future career.

Plenty of fields are open to you, but it is necessary to make a choice. You have hitherto wavered between so many predispositions to this or that profession, that I am quite at a loss to know what you will ultimately decide upon.

So systematically weigh all the ' Pros ' and ' Cons,' and make up your mind for once and all, and let me know.

You must see for yourself that it is no good to go on vacillating between one thing and another, and then finally to make up your mind all in a moment.

Hoping to hear something really definite from you soon.

Your loving mother,

ELIZABETH MARRIOTT.

From a wife to her
husband informing
him of her own
illness *Ash Grove, Sedley,*
10th May 18—

My dearest Husband,

     You will be grieved to hear
that I am far from well, indeed I am
keeping my bed by the doctor's orders.
He does not say what is the matter with
me, but is coming in to see me again this
evening.

I have written to ask my sister Lucy
to come to-morrow to look after things,
so you must not worry.

How I wish you were at home.

          Your loving wife,

             MARIE.

To a husband
informing him of the
illness of a child. *23 Wentworth Park,*
Ashbourne, 11th May 18—

My dearest Husband,

     I fear I have but bad news for
you this letter. Our poor little Harry
is very ill indeed, with a fever tempera-
ture and violent sickness. I have sent
for Dr ——. He will be here directly.

Do you think you could come home
a day earlier ?

Of course, if Harry is worse I shall
telegraph.

          Your unhappy wife,

             NELLY.

To a husband,
asking forgiveness
for having been
ill-tempered *Meadowlands,*
13th May 18—

My ever dear Phil,

     I am about as miserable as I
can be—and I deserve it for my ill-
temper this morning.

How could I have let you go without

even saying good-bye ! But all my foolish temper is over, and only repentance and shame remains.

Forgive me, dear, and when you return you shall find how good I will be. Do send a word of comfort and forgiveness,

To your bad-tempered but loving wife,
NELLY.

To a husband asking him to return home soon

*Rowan House,
York, 13th May* 18—

My own dear Tom,

You told me to let you know if I found myself too dull without you; well, the last few days have been like years, and long ones at that !

Indeed I don't think I can really stand a whole fortnight without you. So do try and come a few days earlier and console

Your disconsolate wife,
JESS.

To a niece, advising her to break off her engagement

*Trafalgar Cottage,
Derby, Feb. 2nd,* 18—

My dearest Niece,

I have a most painful task to derform in writing you this letter, but your dear mother in her last hours begged me to do all I could to fill her place to you. And you will do me the justice, won't you, of acknowledging that I have always done my best to fulfil the sacred promise I then gave ?

It is of Harold Bruce that I have to speak. My dear girl, you are utterly and blindly deceived in him, and however painful it may be to you now, your

only chance of happiness is to break off
the engagement. He is heavily in debt,
both to tradespeople and to friends, and
Mr —— informs me that he is never
likely to earn a sufficient income to keep
himself. His habits of intemperance
grow upon him, and he is thoroughly
idle.

Do, my child, give him up at once.

Think what a wretched life you would
be condemning yourself to, and worse
still, possibly poor little children!

Remember marriage *never* reforms a
man who has no strength of will to re-
form himself *before* marriage.

With much love,

Your affectionate aunt,

PHŒBE LYNDON.

Letter from a **mother to her** **son at school**	*Farley Heath,* *6th Nov.* 18—

My dearest Boy,

It is with great pleasure and
gratification that your father and I hear of
your excellent progress with your studies.
I am sure you have been trying to carry
out those maxims which you and I talked
of together the night before you went
back to school, and they have stood the
test. And your mother trusts you so
entirely that she has not a doubt those
other principles, with regard to the formation of a manly and noble character
which were talked of that same night,
have not been neglected. Good qualities,
when earnestly tended, grow as easily as
bad ones, though some would tell you
otherwise.

Whatever you do, make *habits* now
which you will not be ashamed of when
you are a man. 'The child is father of
the man,' and whatever you let yourself

55

be now, that you will be in an emphasised form when you are a man.

I am sending you a hamper containing some of the good things of this world, by rail to-day. So you will be able to entertain your special friends on your birthday.

I expect you had a fine time with the fireworks yesterday.

I am busy with plum-puddings—does that not make you hungry?

All love, from your devoted

MOTHER.

Birthday letter to
a mother
Leecroft,
1st Aug. 18—

My dearest Mother,

How glad I am that we have you to congratulate on another birthday! Be sure that though I shall be far from you, yet you will be constantly in my thoughts.

I wish all your children could be with you on this special day, but we are scattered far and wide. But when Xmas comes, we shall, we trust, all meet together in the dear old home. With much love to dear father, and an extra birthday allowance for your dear self.

Your loving daughter,

MATILDA.

Birthday letter to
a father
St Saviour's Gate,
York, 3rd May 18—

My dearest Father,

Many, many happy returns of the day, for all our sakes. May you be spared to us for many a long year to come, to brighten the lives of all around you as you have always done.

I do hope that I may so live that my children may love and revere me as yours do you.—Your loving daughter,

HANNAH.

**Application for
the character of
a cook**

4 Standfort Street,
1st April 18—

Dear Madam,

Jane —— has applied for a situation as cook in my service. She tells me that she was cook in your establishment for four years.

Would you kindly tell me if she is clean, honest, and reliable?

Does she thoroughly understand her duties?

By replying to the above questions you will greatly oblige,—Yours truly,

M. BENSON.

Reply—Favourable.

3 Rutland Gardens,
2nd April 18—

Dear Madam,

Jane —— is leaving me because the place is a little too hard for her, as we keep a great deal of company.

In a quieter place she would do excellently. She is clean, honest, and trustworthy.

Her cooking is first-class.

I am, Madam,—Yours truly,

EDITH MARTIN.

Reply—Unfavourable

3 Rutland Gardens,
2nd April 18—

Dear Madam,

With regard to Jane ——, I can say in her favour that she is an excellent cook. She is honest and clean, and would be all that one could desire, were it not that she is possessed of a very bad temper, which plays havoc in the kitchen. But for this same temper I should undoubtedly have kept her.

Yours truly,
EDITH MARTIN.

Application for character of nursemaid

1 *Foreland Street,*
1st Jan. 18—

Dear Madam,

Hearing from Mary —— that she has been two years in your service as nursemaid, I write to ask you if you consider her a suitable person to undertake the charge of two young children. Is she kind and judicious, and is her influence in general what you can approve?

Believe me, Madam,
Yours truly,
MARY R.

Reply—Favourable.

2 *Endsleigh Place,*
2nd Jan. 18—

Dear Madam,

In reply to your letter in reference to Mary ——, I am happy to say I can honestly recommend her.

She has had three children under her care while with me, the youngest being two years old, and the eldest six. She has taken full charge of them, and has also made many of their clothes. She kept their wardrobe in good condition.

She is patient and cheerful, and you would find her a valuable help in many ways.

She is leaving me because I am reducing my establishment.

Believe me, dear Madam,
Yours truly,
R. SCOTT.

Reply—Unfavourable.

2 *Endsleigh Place*
2nd Jan. 18—

Dear Madam,

With regard to M. —— I may say that she is honest, tidy and methodical, but further than that I cannot go, for to be frank, I do not consider her a

suitable person to be in charge of young children.

For one thing, I have discovered that her method of keeping order in the nursery is to frighten the children.

As soon as I discovered this, I naturally gave her notice.

If your children are old enough not to be influenced in that way, she would in other respects probably suit you.

Yours truly,
R. SCOTT.

Application for post as typist
Mill Bank, Norwood,
15th April 18—

To —— ——

Dear Sir,

Hearing that you are in want of a typist, I venture to offer my services.

I have three years' experience and can give excellent references.

I am, Sir,—Yours truly,
EMILY BERTRAM.

Application for situation as bookkeeper in an office
36 Charles Street,
Manchester, 6th April 18—

To —— ——, Esq.

Sir,

Having seen your advertisement in the —— of to-day, I beg to offer myself as a candidate for the post of bookkeeper in your office.

I understand both single and double entry, and was five years in my last situation, which I left in order that I might find a place nearer home. I can furnish you with good testimonials.

I am twenty-two years of age.

Awaiting your reply,
I am,
Yours obediently,
RACHEL HOLDEN.

**Application for post
as assistant mistress
in a school**
                    32 *Park Road,
                    Herne Hill, 8th April* 18—

Dear Madam,

      Hearing that you have a vacancy in your school for an assistant form mistress, I beg to apply for it.

I have matriculated at London, after which I went to Cambridge for two terms, but had most unwillingly to leave on account of my father's money losses.

In addition to the usual English subjects, I can teach botany and zoology, also elementary physiology, and chemistry. I enclose testimonials.

      Believe me,
        Dear madam,
          Yours truly,
          HENRIETTA MICHELJOHN.

**Application for place
as assistant in a
shop**
                    2 *Grove Villas,
                    East Dulwich, 10th April* 18—

Dear Sir,

      In answer to your advertisement, I am applying for a situation as assistant in your shop.

I have had three years' experience in Messrs —— —— establishment, and can give good references.

      I am, Sir,
        Yours obediently,
          HONOR WILSON.

**Application for
situation as lady's
help**
                    1 *Princes Street,
                    Clapham, 2nd April* 18—

Dear Madam,

      Seeing your advertisement in the ——, I beg to offer myself as Lady Help.

Though I have never occupied such a position, I nevertheless feel sure I could

fill it to your satisfaction, as I am thoroughly domesticated and a good needlewoman. I am eighteen years of age, and have excellent health.

Our vicar, the Rev. ——, has kindly allowed me to give his name as a reference.

Awaiting your reply.

> Believe me,
>> Dear Madam,
>>> Yours truly,
>>>> MABEL YATES.

Application for situation as chambermaid

> 12 *Hill Street,*
> *Norwood,* 11*th April* 18—

Madam,

I see by this morning's *Daily News* that you want a chambermaid.

I left my last situation a week ago. I was there five years, and my late mistress tells me she can give me a good character. I am twenty-five years of age, five feet in height, and strong and healthy. I should like £— a year, and my washing paid for.

> I am, Sir,
>> Yours respectfully,
>>> ANN OSBURN.

Application for situation as lady's maid

> 4 *Maiden Hill,*
> *Hanley,* 12*th April* 18—

Madam,

I beg to offer myself as lady's maid, as I hear you are needing one.

I can give a good reference from my last mistress, with whom I lived for four years.

I understand dressmaking and hairdressing, and all the duties required of me.

> I am, Madam,
>> Yours respectfully,
>>> ELIZABETH WESTON.

61

Application for position of music teacher

Mozart Villa,
Ealing, 5th April 18—

Dear Madam,

   Should you require a visiting music-mistress in the school which you advertise to be opened this month, I have pleasure in informing you that I have one day a week not filled up as yet.

I may say that my pupils have been most successful, both in the mechanical and theoretical parts of music. I may add that I give lessons on all stringed instruments, as well as the piano.

   Believe me,
     Dear Madam,
       Yours obediently,
        NORA KAUFMANN.

Application for situation as companion

1 *Ashchurch Road,*
Brixton, 3rd April 18—

Dear Madam,

   Having learnt that you are in need of a companion, I venture to offer my services.

I am twenty-eight years of age, of a cheerful disposition, and have uniformly good health.

I am fond of reading aloud, and am very musical. I can send you excellent references.

   Believe me,
     Dear Madam,
       Yours truly,
        MARIA WILKS.

Application for position of dancing-mistress

Straus Villa,
Finchley, 4th April 18—

Dear Madam,

   Hearing that there is a vacancy in your school for a dancing-mistress, I venture to offer my services.

I am visiting-mistress at the York College for girls, also at Westhill College. In addition to the ordinary course of dancing I teach skirt-dancing and other fancy dances. I have been particularly successful in these latter departments.

Believe me,
Dear Madam,
Yours obediently,
VERENA LENOIR.

Application for situation
as teacher of
drawing
                    10 *West Street,*
                Eastbourne, 9th April 18—

Dear Madam,
            From your advertisement I gather that you wish for a resident drawing-mistress.

I am wishful to obtain such a situation.

I have seven years' experience, and my pupils have succeeded well in examinations at South Kensington and elsewhere. I enclose testimonials.

Yours truly,
MILDRED MOXON.

Application for
post of private
secretary
                    20 *Rupert Street,*
                Maidstone, 7th April 18—

To —— ——, Esq.
Dear Sir,
            In answer to your advertisement for a private secretary, I beg to offer myself as a candidate for the post.

I know shorthand well, am a good typist, and am quick and methodical.

I am, Sir,
Yours respectfully,
SARAH YATES.

2 *Elsmere Road,*
Dulwich, 10*th June* 18—

To Messrs Ridesdale & Coppin.

Gentlemen,

Having seen your advertisement in the *Daily Telegraph*, I venture to offer myself for the situation of clerk.

I have had eighteen months' experience in the house of Messrs ——, and they have kindly offered to testify to my qualifications for the post I desire.

I am twenty years of age, and have always been punctual and methodical.

My present salary is ——.

I am, Gentlemen,

Yours faithfully,

CLARA MAYER.

Application for situation
as companion to a
lady

16 *Morton Terrace,*
Bayswater, 14*th Aug.* 18—

To Mrs ——.

Madam,

In reply to your advertisement in the *Times* of to-day, I beg to offer myself for the situation named.

I am a widow and childless. My disposition is cheerful, and I am a good musician. I am considered a good reader, and have a knowledge of French and German, acquired abroad.

I am accustomed to the management of house and servants, and should not object to travel.

Nursing I am competent to undertake, at all events as regards ordinary

64

illnesses.   Enclosed are some references,
and I can send you others if needed.

> Awaiting your reply,
>> I am, Madam,
>>> Yours truly,
>>>> AGNES BLOUNT.

**From a mother offering
her daughter as
nursery-maid**
> 3 *Leigh Street,*
> *Worthing,* 15*th April* 18—

Madam,

Hearing that you are requiring
a young girl to assist in the nursery, I
beg to offer my daughter.

She has had a year's experience in a
situation where a head nurse was kept,
and her mistress is willing to give her a
good character.

> Awaiting your reply,
>> I am, Madam,
>>> Yours respectfully,
>>>> CHARLOTTE HOBBS.

**Application for
situation as
housekeeper**
> 2 *Meadow Villas,*
> 7*th July* 18—

Sir (or Madam),

Learning from your advertisement in the *Chronicle* of ——, that you
require a housekeeper, I venture to offer
myself for a candidate for the situation.

I am unmarried, and have had a wide
and varied experience, and can without
boasting say that I thoroughly understand the duties which are involved in
such a position of trust, and will con-
scientiously do my best to fulfil them.

I am forty-two years of age, am blessed
with excellent health, and understand
the nursing of any ordinary case of
illness.

The lady whose house I have taken
entire management of for the last two

years has recently died, which is why I am now looking for a new situation.

Awaiting your reply,

Believe me,

Yours obediently,

MARY STUBBS.

From a governess in answer to an advertisement

Madam,

Seeing by your advertisement in the —— that you are in want of a governess for your children, I beg to state that I am leaving my present situation owing to the family having decided to go abroad.

I have been three years with Mrs B——, and she expresses herself quite willing to answer any questions you may like to ask as to my character and my competency to fill the post of teacher of children.—Awaiting your reply,

I am, Madam,

Yours obediently,

MARY G.

Reply—favourable— to application for character of governess

Litham,
4th June 18—

Dear Madam,

In reply to your letter with reference to Miss G——, I may say that during the three years that she has been governess in my family, I have found her uniformly faithful to her duties, and most kindly in her attitude to my children. Her teaching is of a very high order, and her manners in the home are all that can be desired.

She is leaving me because **we are**

going to live abroad, and she prefers strongly to live in England.

I shall be very pleased to give you any special information you may desire.

Yours truly,

MARY D.

Reply—Unfavourable

Litham,
4th June 18—

Dear Madam,

In reply to your letter in reference to Miss G——, I wish to be entirely frank with you, as it is so I should wish to be treated in like case.

Miss G——, then, is an admirable teacher, and my children have made excellent progress while under her care. She is also very kind to children. She has one fault, however, which, if properly dealt with from the beginning, might not prove a serious drawback. She is apt to make unpleasantness with the servants.

We should not have parted with her, however, except that we are going to live abroad, and she prefers to remain in England.—Yours truly,

MARY D.

Letter asking the character of a servant

8 *Russel Square,*
18*th Feb.* 18—

Dear Madam,

Helen B., who states that she has been nine months in your service, has applied for a situation as housemaid in my establishment. Would you kindly tell me if you found her neat, clean, and honest while in your service, whether she is quick and civil, and if she thoroughly understands her duties?

An early reply will greatly oblige.

Yours truly,

M. MASON.

Reply—Favourable

10 *Cheland Gardens*,
19*th Feb*. 18—

Dear Madam,

In reply to your letter in reference to Helen B., I have pleasure in stating that she is clean, quick, and honest, and while in my service performed her duties in every way satisfactorily.

The only thing against her is, that she is not very strong, so could not undertake a hard place.

Believe me,
Yours truly,
Emma Bourke.

Reply—Unfavourable

10 *Cheland Gardens*,
19*th Feb*. 18—

Dear Madam,

In reply to your letter in reference to Helen B., I am sorry to say I cannot thoroughly recommend her. She understands her duties well, is honest and clean, but she is so slow about her work, and in spite of all we can do will not rise early. She is also much given to wasting her time in gossip.

If these faults could be remedied, she would be found an excellent servant.

Yours truly,
Emma Bourke.

**Asking for a
lover's portrait**

5 *Princes Street*,
Matlock, 1*st June* 18—

My dearest Tom,

You were asking me the other day what I should like for my birthday gift, and I teased you by asking for all sorts of impossible things. But now I am going to ask you for something I *really* want, and the possession of which would give me much pleasure.

To come straight to the point, I want your portrait : not one I have already seen, for none of them do you justice (on second thoughts I think I ought not to have written that last phrase in case it might make you conceited—but let it stand!)

And will you indulge a whim of mine and have the photo. taken in your boating suit? and so give the more pleasure to

> Your loving
> NINA.

Letter acknowledging the photo.

. *5 Princes Street,*
Matlock, 6th June 18—

My dearest Tom,

The photo. has just arrived, and what a beautiful silver frame you have put it in!

I expect you won't like my remarking upon the frame before the portrait. This latter is just as good as she who loves you best can desire. You have donned the boating suit too, and what is better, the expression I like best—frank, honest and tender.

> Ever so many thanks,
> From your loving
> NINA.

Birthday letter to a lover

Millbank,
Walsall, 3rd September 18—

My dearest Edwin,

To-morrow is your birthday, so as we shall not see each other, I must send you a special letter to wish you every happiness and success in the coming year.

I am conceited enough to think the

day itself will not be so very happy, as we do not spend it together, and I cannot bring myself to wish it otherwise, which, I suppose, is selfishness on my part. Still it will be happier than your last birthday, when, as you told me, you were wretched because you loved me so much, and thought I should never care for you. And all the time I was loving you in secret.

So think of that and of Monday next, when you will again be with

Your loving

MAY.

Letter to lover complaining of coldness

Ivy Lodge,
7th May 18—

Dear Frank,

After we parted last night I went at once to my own room—but not to sleep. I sat far into the night thinking over our relations, and this letter is the result of my vigil.

A fool's paradise is to my mind a poor dwelling-place indeed! and I, for one, could never live in it. I cannot go on blindly trusting when my senses are wide awake and tell me I have nothing to trust in.

I cannot say that you have omitted any customary attentions to me. But these attentions have become woefully mechanical.

If your old love for me is dead, why trouble to offer me its pitiful corpse in exchange?

Ah! Frank, how short-lived has been that passionate love of yours. Only six short months ago your impatience knew no bounds, if I were absent from you a few moments longer than you expected. You forsook old habits, old friends—

all—just to be with me. You often rode miles through wind and rain—dinnerless, even just to hold my hand in yours for a brief space.

Now the old habits—old friends—and even new ones, form an easy excuse for absence from me, and your visits become rarer and shorter as time goes on.

Well! I would not hold an unwilling lover by the tether of a regretted promise—so you are free.

But another time make quite sure of your own heart and of your own power of unchangeability before you try to win the heart of a woman.

Do not trouble to reply, for my resolve is quite unchangeable.

MARGARET.

**Letter to a
lover**
*Hartover,
7th May 18—*

My dear William,

I really think we shall have to meet less often, for after you have been to see me, for days I can't settle to work. I live over again all the delightful times we have had together, and do what I will, my thoughts will centre themselves on you. Then I begin to be angry with myself. You know my contempt for the woman who sits with her hands in her lap and 'moons' or spends her time in skimming novels! Women ought to work as well as men, both for health of body and mind. If more of them did so, we should hear less about uncomfortable homes and invalid wives.

You sometimes laugh at my theories and ideals, albeit good naturedly, but if they should make me a better wife and a truer companion to you in that happy future we both look forward to, you will not regret them.

71

But if after all I should fail to be all I want to be, I know I can still trust to your love to help and not reproach me.

Your loving
NELL.

From a young lady to her lover who has been urging an immediate marriage

Melton,
19 *May* 18—

Dear Alfred,

I have read your letter over many times, and I must say the reasons you urge for our immediate marriage are none of them nearly as strong as those I can bring forward for a further delay.

As you know, since my father had that accident to his eyes, I have been doing much writing for him, and the doctors say he ought not to use them for at least three months. Then the worry and anxiety about father has worn out my mother, and she much needs what help I can give her with my young brothers and sisters.

Till all this is tided over I know I should be selfish and wicked to leave home. I am sure we cannot hope for happiness in our new life if we begin it by neglecting duty, and for the present my duty lies at home.

Have patience, a few months will soon pass, and we shall be in our own little home before winter comes.

Think over your letter again and unsay some of it. I want to feel that when we are married you will influence me to do my duty and not to neglect it.

The photo. of yourself, which I got by the same post as your letter, is excellent, and it just fits the silver frame you gave me on my birthday. The lanes are looking lovely, now the hawthorn is

out.   When you come on Saturday
bring your cycle and we can go for a
nice long run.   I have not been further
than the garden for a week, so it will be
delightful to get an afternoon in the
country lanes, and I shall arrange my
work so that I can be free then.

Yours as ever,
MILLIE.

From a lady whose
lover has been
neglecting her and
paying attentions to
another

Holmwood,
1st Aug. 18—

Dear Henry,

For a long time I have been
unwillingly under the impression that
you have been growing tired of me.

I tried to think that your mind was
absorbed in your work so much that
you had not the leisure to pay me those
little attentions which were so pleasant
to me during the first months of our
engagement.   But although I did feel
the difference in your manner very much,
I hid my disappointment, and I am sure
you never found me complaining about
anything, for I know how disagreeable
an exacting woman must be to a man.
But now I feel that silence on my part
would be a wrong alike to you and
myself, for I hear that during the time
last week when I believed you to be
deep in law books, you were, in fact, up
the river with the Browns, and I am
informed were paying marked attention
to Nellie.

All this proves that my early sus-
picions that you were tiring of me were
but too well founded, but it would have
been more manly on your part had you
been frank enough to tell me of your

altered feelings, instead of letting me learn it so unpleasantly from an outsider.

I now most willingly give you back your freedom, and am only too thankful that I have discovered what manner of man you are before I was tied to you for ever.

Yours sincerely,
MABEL THURTON.

Letter from a servant to her lover

Maitland House,
3rd April 18—

My dearest Tom,

Your letter reached me last Thursday, but we have had so much company that I have not had a minute to myself, so I could not write till to-day.

You ask me if we can't be married in August? Well, I think not, for neither of us has money enough to get a nice home by then, and mother always said if young people didn't get things before they were married, they never got them after. There are so many things wanted in a house that a man never thinks of, and the great thing is to start fair.

By waiting we shall get things so much more comfortable.

But we shall see each other soon, for my mistress says I shall have a week's holiday in May when the spring cleaning is done.

I am glad I am going then, as Amy will be at home, and it will be the first time we have been home together since we both went to service.

With best love,
Your affectionate
MATILDA.

Another

My dear Harry,

I am very sorry to tell you that I cannot have my night out this week, so that I shan't see you till Sunday evening.

The reason is this. My fellow-servant's mother was taken ill suddenly, and my mistress had to let her go home to look after her till Saturday, when her sister will take her place.

I am the more sorry not to see you as I wanted to talk to you about leaving your situation. Don't you think you can try and stay on? You are getting good money, and you can never hope to get a place where there is nothing to put up with. I am sure it does no one any good to keep on changing places. It unsettles anyone all round. You have lost seven weeks' work already this year through changing, and all this makes the time further off when we can get our little home together.

I am doing my part, and have got together most of the household linen, which I have made in the evenings with the sewing machine I bought last winter. I make my own dresses, too, which saves me a little money, and I am getting on well. But it takes the heart out of me when I keep hearing that you are out of a place.

It is getting late, and I am tired with having had extra work the last day or two, so I will conclude with best love, and am,

Your loving
E LIZA.

To a lover expressing a change of feeling

Rose Villa,
21st June 18—

My dear Andrew,

It is with pain and humiliation that I sit down to write this letter, and my task is all the harder because you have always treated me with such genuine kindness and consideration, and I have a great respect for you.

But this very respect makes it impossible for me to sail under false colours, and do you the grievous wrong of marrying you when I cannot feel that I can give you that whole-hearted love which a wife should give to a husband.

I feel that I have done you a wrong in engaging myself to you, until I knew my own heart better, but I should do you a much greater wrong were I to marry you, feeling as I do.

So I must ask you to release me from my promise, and forgive me if you can for the pain I know I shall cause you. I do hope that you will soon find someone more worthy of your unselfish love than

Your sincere friend,
MARGARET SMITH.

From a lady to her lover fixing the marriage day

11 *Monmouth Square,*
1st June 18—

My dear John,

You ask me to name the day for our marriage.

My mother and I think 21st July would be the most suitable time, because my brother Fred would then be back from Ireland. Would that date suit you? We have both looked forward so gladly to the time when we should never be parted, and yet now that my new life is really on the eve of beginning, I

76

feel depressed and unhappy. Believe
me it is not that my affection for you is
in any way lessened, but my old life
which has been so happy will be all over,
and I shall begin a new life which will
be all strange. And I am haunted by
the fear, lest you will be disappointed
in me when you have me always with
you. I shall be sure to make mistakes
at first, before I have become accustomed
to my new responsibilities, possibly annoying ones to a man. But have
patience with me, for I shall try so
earnestly to make your home bright and
happy.

Aunt Hannah sent me to-day all my
household linen, and Uncle Robert a
silver tea and coffee service; so it does
begin to feel like getting married.

I shall be the first of the birds to leave
the nest—that is mother's remark.

With all love,

SARAH.

**Answer to letter
proposing marriage—
Unfavourable** 1 *Monmouth Street*,
10*th April* 18—

Dear Sir,

I thought from my manner of
receiving your smallest attentions, that
it would have been evident to you that
those same attentions were disagreeable
to me. You will do me the justice to
acknowledge that I never on any single
occasion gave you the least encourage-
ment.

Hoping you will come to your senses,
and forget me as soon as possible.

I am, yours truly,

MABEL YATES.

**Answer to
proposal of marriage
—Unfavourable**

12 *Newcombe St.*,
2nd June 18—

Dear Mr Jones,

It is not a mere form of words when I say I am deeply grieved by the receipt of your letter. Firstly, because I like you and believe in your sincerity. Secondly, because I am fearful lest in the friendly intercourse we have had together, I might, without intending it, have led you to think I was disposed to favour attentions other than those of a purely friendly character.

Such a thought as your caring for me in any deeper sense never entered my mind at any time.

Forget, then, as I will try to do, that you ever penned that letter. I wish to remain your friend,

ANNA SMITH.

**Answer to proposal
of marriage—
Favourable**

12 *Newcombe St.*,
2nd June 18—

Dear Mr Jones,

I cannot say that your letter was altogether a surprise to me, for you possess one, to my mind, admirable quality in man or woman—transparency. This very quality in you, while it showed me you had a character with no need for cupboards in which to secrete skeletons, made me like you from the first. You see I am following your example, and am frank in my turn. One thing I should wish, and that is, that we enter into no formal engagement till we have seen more of each other.

Yours sincerely,
ANNA SMITH.

**Answer to proposal
of marriage—
Favourable**

2 *Strathmore Place,*
3rd July 18—

Dear Fred,
　　　　　We had been playmates and
friends so long, that somehow it never
came into my mind that we might
become something nearer and dearer,
yet when your letter came I found that
for you to go away to another country,
and for me possibly never to see you
again, would be unbearable.

Perhaps we have loved each other all
along without suspecting it.

I know my parents would wish nothing
better than that we should marry, though
that we shall have to live so far away
will necessarily be a trouble to them.

I will write no more, as we meet on
Monday.

MARGARET.

**Answer to proposal
of marriage—
Unfavourable**

1 *Rutland Square,*
3rd Aug. 18—

Dear Mr Unwin,
　　　　　I am quite sensible of the
honour you do me in asking me to
marry you, and I thank you for the
many kind expressions contained in
your letter.

But I have long since made up my
mind never to leave my poor mother,
who depends upon me so completely
since her health failed.

I may say that no selfish reason can
ever bring me to change my resolution.

Hoping you may find a wife worthy of
you, and one who will make you happy.

Believe me,
　　　　Yours sincerely,
　　　　　　JANE GIBBS.

79

Answer to proposal
of marriage from a
man who is a flirt   *Carendon House,*
                    1st May 18—

Dear Sir,

      You may not be aware that
Miss Watson is a great friend of mine,
and that in consequence I read your
letter to her in March last.

It was infinitely amusing to find the
same expressions repeated in your letter
to me that you had used to her.

I wonder how many more such letters
you have written?

Please do not reply to this, as I
have no wish to hear of or from you
again.

        Yours truly,
          Emma Yates.

From a young
lady to a friend   *Hazlewood,*
                    17th June 18—

My dear Martha,

      I have just got my heart's
desire, viz.—a sewing machine, and I
have spent the morning in unravelling
its mysteries. I got into some delightful
muddles at first, but now I think I shall
get on all right.

I have bought some patterns, both
flat and made-up, so you see I mean
business.

The first thing I am going to undertake
is a muslin blouse, and if that turns out all
right, I shall make up that lovely piece
of silk which Aunt Mary gave me. For
a time (until the novelty wears off,
father says), the country lanes I have
so persistently haunted since I took to
cycling will know me no more.

How goes your music? Do you still
worship at Beethoven's shrine? Yesterday I tried over the No. 2 Nocturne of

Chopin—it is simply lovely. But I shall never shine very brilliantly in music, as they used to say of me at school. I never could bring myself to work at scales and exercises, as you will well remember.

Do you think you could come to us for a fortnight in August? Do if you possibly can, for we are going to have a capital time then, what with garden-parties, picnics and boating.

Ada will be home from France then.

With much love,

Always your loving friend,

ANNIE.

Reply to same

Whitby,
20th June 18—

My dear Annie,

Your letter came in the very nick of time, for a family council was being held here about holiday arrangements for August, and I was all but booked for Scotland. Now I am glad to say I can accept your kind invitation.

I long for the time to come. I expect you will have a whole wardrobe of dainty toilets to make me envious now that you have that long-desired sewing-machine, and I shall have to rack my brains in search of becoming novelties, unless I mean to be put into the shade altogether!

One thing I have done to add to my attractions—namely, altering the style of doing my hair. They all here think it a great improvement. My impertinent brother informs me that it softens down my somewhat too pronounced features!

Whitby is looking lovely now, and we nearly live out of doors.

Yesterday we got up a picnic to Robin Hood's Bay, and had a delightful time.

We spoke of you, and wished you were with us.

We are going to have another Bazaar in July in aid of a new organ for our church, and mother and I have to take a stall.

Now, do be a good girl and help us! Remember you have that sewing-machine now!

I think I have exhausted my news for the moment, so conclude with love, and am,

Your affectionate friend,
MARTHA.

From a young lady to a friend announcing her engagement
2 Milton Place,
26th Oct. 18—

My dear Maggie,

Remembering our old compact that whichever of us became engaged to be married should let the other know at once, I write to tell you that George Wilson asked me yesterday to be his wife, and I consented. Mother and father are delighted.

We are both so happy, and George is going to stay here over the week-end.

Our proverbial 'fly' in the pot of honey is that that wretched little imp of a brother of mine imagines we can't be happy without his society, and haunts us presistently. George gives him choco-altes to run away and play with, and he swallows them with a rapidity which I tell him is most greedy and rude, and comes back and squats down and regards us. To think that until yesterday I looked upon him as a cherub!

Are you fond of playing 'gooseberry'? If so, come and see

Your fortunate friend,
BERTHA.

To procure admission of a girl into a school

Weston-super-Mare,
30th April 18—

To Mr Alderman B———.

My dear Sir,

You, I know, will have great influence in the city, and I know, too, that your benevolence is so great that I venture to ask you for your influence to further a very good cause.

A word from you would, I feel sure, procure admission to the ——— schools for a little girl whose parents both met their death in the fire which occurred in Princes Street. The poor child has no one at all to look to for help.

Could admission to the ——— schools be obtained, I am sure her future would be assured. She has a good disposition, and is quick and intelligent.

Do if possible help me, and so earn the gratitude both of the child and—

Yours most obediently,
SARAH COLLINS.

Letter to landlord about repairs

Holmewood,
6th March 18—

Dear Sir,

As we have now been over — years in this house, could you not have it painted and papered? It is badly in need of it. Woodwork, walls and ceilings are alike dirty.

The spouting, too, is out of order, so when it rains the walls become very wet, and will be permanently damp if not seen to soon.

Yours truly,
EMMA BATES.

**Reply to announcement
of engagement**
6 *Hanover Square,
York, 17th Oct.* 18—

My dear Bertha,

You can imagine with what interest I read your letter. And you may be sure I most heartily congratulate you, for George Wilson has always been a great favourite of mine (don't be jealous!)

I don't know that 'playing gooseberry' is a most exhilarating occupation, nevertheless I will come and perform that kind office before long.

When must I begin to prepare my bridesmaid toilet?

Your affectionate friend,

MAGGIE.

**Letter wishing friend
a happy birthday**
*The Elms,
Whitby, 1st March* 18—

My dear Ellen,

I cannot let your birthday pass without sending you my congratulations and sincere wishes for your happiness, not only on the day itself, but on all succeeding days.

We are having such boisterous weather here that it is next to impossible to walk on the cliffs. But one must worry through the month somehow, I suppose, and look forward to May.

With much love,

From your old friend,

MARGUERITE.

**Letter asking a
friend to be a
bridesmaid**
*Westland,
Clapham Common, 16th Oct.* 18—

My dear Nelly,

My wedding day is at last fixed, so I now ask you to fulfil your old promise of being a bridesmaid.

We are to be married on 10th November—not a very cheerful month!

Some one will be there whose only subject of conversation seems to be *yourself*. So it would not surprise me if a certain happy 'bridesmaid' was asked to be a 'happy bride!' Do not let this suggestion frighten you into not fulfilling your promise to your old friend,

BELLA WINDALL.

Reply—favourable

3 Church Street,
Nottingham, 17th Oct. 18—

My dear Bella,

Your letter delighted me till I read the last part—this set me quaking, and I can scarcely tell whether with pleasure or pain. I cannot pretend that I do not know to whom you refer. But I shall keep my promise and come.

Your affectionate friend,
NITA GRAHAM.

Reply—Unfavourable

3 Church Street,
Nottingham, 17th Oct. 18—

My dear Bella,

I can't come! and I am so disappointed for more reasons than one. Have I betrayed myself?

I am compelled to go away to the south of France with my mother, who is troubled with her chest again.

Nothing but the fullest account of everything can console

Your loving friend,
NITA GRAHAM.

Letter introducing a friend

Ivy Lodge,
1st Oct. 18—

My dear Mrs Watson,

Will you let me introduce my old college friend Miss Marlow to you?

She will be in town for the next month, and I should like two of my most valued friends to know each other.

If you would send her a card for one of your 'days' I know it would give her pleasure.

She is very musical, which ought to be something to put you in touch at once, and every one considers her a delightful companion.

Once admit her to the nursery and I will answer for it your young folks will contrive to make her a frequent visitor. Her address is 7 Carlton Terrace, West Kensington.

Hoping you are all well and prospering.

Your sincere friend,
ANNA MONMOTII.

Reply

1 *Princes Mansions,*
5th Oct. 18—

My dear Anna,
I called upon Miss Marlow yesterday, and find her altogether charming. To-morrow she will dine with us 'en famille,' so that we can get to know more of each other.

No doubt she will find her way to the nursery, and I do not doubt results since I have seen her.

With affectionate regards,
Yours as ever,
ELIZABETH WATSON.

Letter acknowledging
ordinary present   *The Hollies,*
Maidstone, 4th June 18—

My dearest Aunt,
Imagine my surprise and delight when I opened your parcel, which reached me by this morning's post.

A whole dozen pairs of gloves! and

such nice ones. I really don't know
which pair to wear first, they are all such
pretty shades.

Mother says you will make me extravagant, and that instead of mending
a pair I shall just get out a new one.
Isn't that too bad, when I keep all my
things so neatly mended?

Well, your kind gift shall not be a
means of making me throw aside thrifty
habits.

With much love and many thanks,

Your affectionate niece,

ADA.

Another

West Lodge,
Hastings, 10th *June* 18—

My dear Friend,

Your hamper of fruit and roses
reached me this morning, and I thank
you as much for the kind thought as for
the gift itself.

It is so pleasant to be remembered in
one's loneliness.

My health is gradually improving, but
it is a slow process, requiring a lot of
patience.

I am allowed to read again now, so
time does not hang so heavily as it did.
And the weather being so ideal, allows
of my getting out for a drive sometimes.

Hoping you and all your circle are
quite well and flourishing,

Believe me,

Gratefully yours,

MAUDE BANKS.

With gift of
photograph
The Oaks,
Clapham, 16th *April* 18—

My dearest Elsa,

Although I have a reputation
for not keeping my promises, I fulfil one

to-day by sending you my photograph. Whether it is like me or not is a matter for you to decide.

At home the majority is in its favour, though my young brother, after the manner of his kind, declares that it flatters me. Secretly, I am of his opinion, though outwardly I show some indignation regarding the opinions (particularly the mode of expressing them) of male folks in general, and brothers in particular.

Awaiting your more unbiassed verdict, and with love,

Believe me,

Always your loving friend,

ELLA.

**Acknowledgment
of present** 3 *Nelson Square,*
Richmond, 18th April 18—

My dear Mabel,

How can I thank you enough for the beautiful gift you have sent to me? It is quite the most lovely Indian shawl I have seen, and is of more value inasmuch as it shows that though absent on your travels your friend was not absent from your mind.

Again thanking you,

Always your loving friend,

EVA.

Christmas greeting
Norlands,
Edgbaston, 18th April 18—

My dearest Milly,

This is just a short note to wish you and yours a most joyous Christmastide. I am so glad to think that you will have your family circle complete this Xmas.

Last year Charlie was in France, and I remember how his absence spoiled the

festivities, at least as far as you were concerned.

We shall be all at home, and as Margaret and Elly have not set up their usual Xmas bronchitis, we look for good times ourselves.

The children's Xmas tree is to be quite fine this year. All the children have contributed something made by themselves.

How one lives one's own childhood over again in one's children!

But I must finish, as there are endless things to see to.

So with love and all good wishes,

Always your affectionate

HANNAH.

Letter to uncle asking for loan
The Elms,
Worthing, 1st April 18—

My dearest Uncle,

If this letter isn't a 'begging' one it is next door to it, for I am writing to ask you to lend me £5.

I left my situation last February, and am only just in my new one.

I don't like to ask for an advance on my salary from people who are almost strangers to me, and I must get some summer garments, but mind I won't take a penny unless you let me pay you back. So do, like the dear old uncle you are, make no objection.

With much love,

Your affectionate niece,

MARGARET BARLOW.

To brother asking for a loan
Ivy Cottage,
30th March 18—

Dearest Hal,

Can you lend me two guineas? I have been disgracefully extravagant
89

and spent all my dress allowance, and I really can't ask father for more this month. I am invited for a week to Kingston, and want some more of what you term 'faldelals.'

I will pay you back out of my next allowance, and be ever so good over my money in future.—Your loving sister,

LILLA.

Letter to landlord
who has refused
to have the house
done up

The Lawn,
Brixton, 9th March 18—

Dear Sir,

As we have not renewed the lease of this house, and as you point-blank refuse to have it painted and papered, I write to tell you that we give you notice, and shall leave the premises on the earliest possible date.

Yours truly,
RHODA GREEN.

12 Vincent Road,
Clapham, 10th March 18—

To J. Henchell, Esq.

Dear Sir,

You were so kind as to tell me when my husband died that if you could be of service to me I was to command you. At that time I hoped I should not need to avail myself of what I nevertheless looked upon as a great kindness.

Now, owing to the expense of illness in the family, I do for the moment find myself in need of a £10 note.

If you would kindly lend me that amount for a couple of months you would relieve my mind of much anxiety.

Thanking you in advance,
Believe me,
Sincerely and gratefully yours,
ANN GIBSON.

**Letter to
landlord about
cistern**
*Rose Villa,
Southend, 7th March* 18—

Dear Sir,

Will you kindly send at once
and have our hot-water cistern seen to ?
The present one, which is of worn-out
zinc, runs so that no patching can avail.

It would be much better to replace
with a copper one that will last.

I hope there will be no delay, as, of
course, we can't use the kitchen range,
so are put to great inconvenience.

You have not yet sent to have the side
gate mended as you promised, but that
is not so urgent as the cistern.

Yours truly,
MARION MILWARD.

**Application for
autograph**
*42 Esmond Road,
Hastings, 17th April* 18—

To —— ——

Dear Sir (or Madam),

Being a most sincere admirer
of your writings, may I beg as a favour
that will be appreciated to the full—your
autograph.

Should you feel the smallest compunc-
tion in granting the request of an entire
stranger, I can only ask you to destroy
my letter without giving it another
thought.

But if you should feel disposed to
gratify what is not the mere greed of an
autograph collector, but a wish arising
out of sincere admiration and regard, I
enclose an envelope for the purpose.

Believe me,
Sir (or Madam),
Yours sincerely,
ROSAMUND LEGREY.

**Letter asking for
subscription to a
charity**

*The Hill,
Hastings, 19th May* 18—

To Mrs Broadbent.

Dear Madam,

May I call your attention to a most deserving charity ?

We have just established down here a Holiday Home for the poor little half-starved children at Bethnel Green.

Already we have no fewer than forty-two little ones who are getting their first taste of happiness, of pure air and sufficient food. But in order to work our scheme satisfactorily, we are in urgent need of funds.

If you can help us a little we should indeed be grateful, but we know how widespread is your charity, so it may be that you will feel you cannot add one more to your list of subscriptions.

In any case we offer you a cordial invitation to inspect our ' Home,' and judge for yourself of the work we are trying to do.—I am, dear Madam,

Yours obediently,

EMILY BOND,

(Secretary).

Reply—favourable

*Matherton Hall,
22nd May* 18—

Dear Miss Bond,

I have already heard indirectly of the excellent work you are doing, and I enclose five guineas for the furtherance of your estimable charity.

Yours truly,

EDITH BROADBENT.

Reply—unfavourable

*Matherton Hall,
22nd May* 18—

Dear Miss Bond,

I have already heard of the good and useful work in which you are

engaged, and would gladly add my name to your list of subscribers were it not that the claims upon me are so heavy and so numerous.

Wishing you success,

Yours truly,

EDITH BROADBENT.

Letter asking for
an introduction to
a third party *Norlands,*
5th Nov. 18—

My dear Marion,

I am going to stay at York for a few weeks, and I should so much like to make the acquaintance of your friend Mrs Lisbel, whose poems I admire so much.

If she would not think it an intrusion, would you be so kind as to give me an introduction to her?

Yours sincerely,

HARRIET MASON.

Letter asking lady
to sing at a
concert *The Vicarage,*
Dunstable, 12th Sept. 18—

Dear Miss Elton,

We are getting up a concert in aid of our schools on the 30th; would you be so very good as to let your name appear on our programme?

It would be a great attraction, I can assure you, without flattery, and I hope you will be willing to oblige.

Yours cordially,

HENRIETTA WINTHORPE.

Reply—favourable 3 *York Mansions, W.,*
14th Sept. 18—

Dear Mrs Winthorpe,

I shall be very pleased to sing at your concert on the 30th.

Would it be too much trouble for you

93

to secure my old rooms for me at the Bull Hotel?

You know my weakness in this matter.

Yours very sincerely,

ELLA ELTON.

Reply—unfavourable

3 *York Mansions, W.,*
14th Sept. 18—

Dear Mrs Winthorpe,

I am very sorry indeed to have to refuse to help at your concert. But on the 30th I am singing at Manchester.

Otherwise to have been of use to you would have given much pleasure to

Yours,

ELLA ELTON.

**Letter asking lady
to assist in bazaar
work**

1 *York Place,*
Kensington, 10th *July* 18—

Dear Mrs Davis,

Can you find time to help me with my work for our bazaar? The lovely things you are so skilled in contriving always sell well, and make such an attraction to a stall.

I know if it depends on inclination you will come to my assistance, for I have a fancy stall all to myself this time, which is a serious responsibility, and my sisters having gone abroad, I can get no help from them this time.

The date of the bazaar is 29th August.

With kindest regards,

Yours truly,

MABEL WATSON.

Reply

Weston,
Richmond, 11th *July* 18—

Dear Mrs Watson,

I shall be most happy to assist you with your bazaar, and will

94

see that my contributions reach you in good time.

With kind regards,
Yours very truly,
MARGARET DAVIS.

Birthday letter from a young lady to her former governess

1 *York Place,*
Brighton, 6*th March* 18—

My dearest Friend,

I cannot let your birthday pass without wishing you the time-honoured 'many happy returns of the day,' and asking your kind acceptance of the accompanying purse and volume of poems. I hope your birthday will be a very happy one. I well remember how much you did to make my birthdays happy in the dear old schoolroom days, alas! gone for ever.

I know now, better than in those days, how much I owe to you. And believe me, I am truly grateful.

It seems so long since I saw you; won't you make an effort and come to see

Your affectionate old pupil,
LILIAN STRONG.

Birthday congratulations

1 *Hanover St.,*
4*th Jan.* 18—

My dear Milly,

To-morrow is your birthday, so I cannot let the day pass without offering my sincere congratulations.

I am offering for your kind acceptance a handkerchief-case which it has given me much pleasure to embroider for you. I hope it will reach you safely.

With love and every good wish,
Believe me,
Your loving friend,
ADA.

95

Another to a gentleman

Meadowlands,
9th April 18—

My dear Tom,

Will you accept the accompanying pair of slippers as an expression of affection from Norah and myself? We have each worked one, so it is a genuinely conjoint affair. You will see by this that though separated by time and distance, you have still a tender place in our memory.

You will be glad to hear that we are all well. Mother has ceased to be an invalid, and, indeed, seems as bright and youthful as the best of us. Father begins to have a sprinkling of silver among his brown curls, and Harry is positively beginning to shave!

All join me in love and birthday wishes.

Your loving cousin,
ROSE.

To a friend who is ill

Ivy Cottage,
10th June 18—

My dear Janet,

I cannot tell you how truly I am grieved to hear of your illness. It is indeed hard lines to be a prisoner in this lovely June weather. You must be lonely too, since your sister has left you! I only wish I could come and install myself in your home till you are better, but alas! I am fettered by duties which only I can properly fulfil, and must, for some time at least, remain here.

I am, however, sending you some friends who will never obtrude themselves without your desire—who will never be noisy, or contradict—or do any of the things many mere flesh and blood friends do when one is ill. To cease my 'funning,' I am sending a parcel of new

books. I know you can never get
enough to read, unless you have greatly
changed, and I know, too, that in such
an out-of-the-way place as your present
abode, books are not easy to get.

Hoping soon to hear better news of
you,

Always your friend,
MABEL WHITHAM.

Answer to same

Celmore Crags,
12th June 18—

My dear Mabel,

   Your cheery note and welcome
parcel of books reached me yesterday,
and I am more than grateful for your
kindly thought.

Indeed I was in a state of book-starva-
tion until the advent of that parcel, and
was reduced to falling back on some old
'Spectators.'

Now I am going to indulge in a
regular debauch of reading, so time will
not drag so with me.

As you say, it is hard to be a prisoner
in this lovely June weather, especially
for any one who revels in an outdoor life
as I do.

From the window near which my
couch is placed I have a full view of my
garden, and the very flowers seem to
cry out for me.

Well! patience! and soon I shall don
garden hat and gloves and look to my
nurslings again.

In the meantime a thousand thanks
from

Your friend,
JANET.

From a lady asking
a friend for information
about gas-stoves   *The Eagles,*
                  Brixton, 2nd Sept. 18—

My dear Hilda,

As winter is coming on, the domestic difficulty of fires once more presents itself, and as I know you made a trial of gas-stoves last winter, I am writing to ask you the result of your experiment. If you find it has proved satisfactory I shall probably follow your example.

Will you tell me, first, if there is any smell when the stove is burning; secondly, does a gas fire look nice and cheerful; and lastly, does it cost more than an ordinary fire ?

I know you won't mind the trouble of sending a reply as soon as possible to

Your sincere friend,

DOROTHY.

Reply to same
                  Alma House,
            West Dulwich, 4th Sept. 18—

My dear Dorothy,

I have much pleasure in giving you the information you desire.

I have found gas-stoves a great blessing, I can assure you. The saving in labour and in dirt is enormous, making nearly the difference of a servant. Last winter I kept one servant less than before, only having a woman in to help half the day on Saturdays.

The rooms don't get dusty and curtains don't get dirty. Then it is so pleasant to come down in the cold morning and not have to breakfast by a coal fire, which the housemaid assures you blandly is 'getting up nicely,' though by appearance it is a layer of burnt paper, a few

98

bits of charred wood and a sickly tongue of flame!

Ask me anything else that occurs to you.

As to cost, the extra gas is quite made up for in other ways.

Yours affectionately,

HILDA.

Requesting a friend
to look for lodgings
at the seaside *New Barnet,*
12th July 18—

My dear Milly,

Your letter conveys such a glowing account of Liscombe Bay, that I have decided to go there with the children.

Would you mind finding me some lodgings as near you as possible? The house you are in is, you say, full, so there is no hope of my getting rooms there.

I shall require two bedrooms and a sitting-room, with attendance. I should prefer a house which has a bathroom, but that is not an essential, as I could bring my folding-bath.

But oh! do be sure the drains have been tested, as I have such a horror of bad drains, remembering my experience of last year.

Should you be able to find me a place, I will come next week. Until then—With love,

I am,

Yours affectionately,

LILIAN MOSS.

Reply to same

2 Royal Terrace,
Liscombe Bay, 14th *July* 18—

My dear Lilian,

I have found rooms that I think may meet your requirements.

They are not as near my own as I could desire, but Liscombe is so full just now, that you are fortunate to get anything. The two bedrooms communicate, but that I know will be no objection, and the sitting-room commands a fine view of the Bay.

The price of the rooms is £—— per week.

Wire to me if I am to engage them, or they may be taken. I am delighted to think of your coming.

Yours affectionately,
MILLY WEST.

From a lady to a friend asking for advice

North Parade,
Weston, 4th May 18—

My dear Emma,

You are so encyclopædic in your knowledge of things, that I want to trespass upon your kindness so far as to ask your advice about various matters.

Firstly, then—you know how I pride myself on my lovely lace , well, it is disgracefully treated at the laundry, and my housemaid, who has tried her hand at it, does it infinitely worse! so I have resolved to do it myself. Can you give me a few hints?

Now to the next point. Do you consider bicycling good for girls? Mary and Eva are frantic to have one, and I am disposed to yield to their importunities if it will add to their bodily well-being as much as to their enjoyment.

I hope your holiday has blown away the cobwebs, as you express it, and that you feel your old vigorous self again.

We are all well, I am glad to say, and as the weather is so delightful we get out a great deal.

Hoping you won't think me a bore for worrying you about my affairs, and with love to all your circle,

Believe me,

Your sincere friend,

AMY NORRIS.

Reply

Hillborough,
Buxton, 10th May 18—

My dear Amy,

Of course I am delighted to be of use to you in any way, so always command me.

Now about the lace. You are doing a wise thing in undertaking it yourself, as it certainly does want careful treatment, and laundresses have not time to give the necessary attention when disposed to do it.

Get a large glass bottle and cover it with folds of flannel. Wrap the lace evenly round the bottle and give both ends a tack.

Now make a warm soapy lather with curd soap, and dip the bottle up and down in it, gently pressing the lather to the lace with the hand until quite clean. Then rinse in cold water. If the lace is very fine do not iron it at all, but pull it gently into shape, and place it between sheets of white blotting-paper, and put a heavy weight on it.

This is quite the best method for Honiton or any expensive lace.

Now about the bicycle. Certainly let Mary and Eva ride. It will do them heaps of good.

I am expecting visitors, so please excuse more for this time from

Your affectionate friend,

EMMA MOORE.

From a lady who
has experienced a
sudden reverse of
fortune
Manor House,
Elsleigh, 30th Oct. 18—

My dear Maria,

A most dreadful calamity has
befallen us in the breaking of —— Bank.

We shall only have money left to live
in the most economical fashion now. I
could bear it for myself, but it tortures
me to see my dear husband so broken
down. And my poor girls, who are just
at an age to be brought out too!

But for the sake of the others, I am
determined to look resolutely on the
bright side. I tell myself how much
better it is that the blow should have
fallen when the children are educated
and properly brought up. Also is it not
a blessing that we are one and all in
good health?

You remember the little cottage we
bought last year in Surrey? Well, it is
there that we shall go to live, and let
this house. The rent will be a considerable help to us.

We are going to have a sale of all the
furniture, as none of it will be suitable
for our cottage.

The horses and carriages are all to go
except the little white pony; that we
shall keep as we have a stable at the
cottage, and there are some lovely drives
we could take to cheer our spirits.

My under housemaid has consented to
come as a general servant; one of the
grooms, too, is coming as 'general facto-
tum.'

I cannot write more, for the girls and
I have to go through all our possessions,
and pack, and have removed such things
as we desire to keep.—With love,

I am,— Your unfortunate friend,

EDITH M^CLEOD.

To a friend who has experienced a reverse of fortune

Oak Cottage,
1st Nov. 18—

My dear Edith,

I knew through the newspapers about the breaking of —— Bank before your sad letter reached me, and my heart bled for you.

It is indeed a dreadful change for you to make in your mode of life. But you who have so well stood the test of riches, will, I know, bear your reverses bravely. There is a bright side to your misfortune, for you have enough left you to live simply upon, and I can tell you for your consolation that though you will be deprived of many luxuries, still you will lose many cares which riches involve.

I have always had to practise economy, as you know, so I daresay I shall be able to give you some useful hints. Believe me, my dear friend, all this sounds much harder than it really is when put into actual practice, and I can picture you in your pretty cottage, acknowledging that after all you are more truly happy than when at the Manor.

Do let me know if I can be of any help to you in any way, for no one would be more glad to be a comfort to you than

Your affectionate friend,

MARIA.

From one lady to another, whom she believes to be the victim of a misunderstanding

Alexandra House,
Nottingham, 3rd March 18—

Dear Matilda,

As you have sent no reply to my last two letters I begin to fear that I have in some way offended you. I

assure you that if this is the case, it has been quite unintentional on my part. I have too much genuine regard for you ever to give you pain knowingly.

Do write to me quite frankly, and I will reply in the same spirit.

From your sincere friend,
ANNIE DAVIS.

Reply to same

Newark,
4th March 18—

My dear Annie,

I am so sorry you should have been made uneasy by my silence. I know you too well, and indeed am not so foolish as to get offended and choose silence as a means of expressing my ruffled sentiments.

The reason is simply this: my servants all gave notice in a body, when they learnt that my husband's mother was to come to live with us, and as I have only just been able to replace them, and that unsatisfactorily, you may imagine I have not had a moment to sit down and write.

As soon as we are a little less at sixes and sevens you shall have a long letter.

From your sincere friend,
MATILDA WHITE.

From a lady who is anxious to interest another in a poor girl

Hartlepool,
29th Aug. 18—

Dear Mrs Price,

Knowing from long experience your charitable large-heartedness, I want to ask your kind interest in a most estimable young woman, who is much in need of help. Her father (a saddler by trade) has suddenly died, leaving her with two children entirely dependent on

104

her, the eldest being nine years old, and
the youngest a baby of two years, whose
mother died at its birth. Esther Gill
(that is her name) is a very clever needlewoman, and if you could give her a little
work she would do it well.

Also, if you have any of your children's
clothes which are done with, I should be
so glad if you would let her have them,
for the poor girl will find it hard to
make both ends meet.

Thanking you in advance,
Believe me,
Yours sincerely,
NORAH GREEN.

Letter to a young
lady who is going to
marry a missionary—
From a school
friend   *Holmleigh,*
                           7th May 18—

My dear Anna,
          On receipt of your letter, my
feelings were of a mingled character.
Uppermost perhaps was a feeling of
sorrow that in the future we shall be
separated by so great a distance.

Still, I am happy to think that you
will be married to a good man, and one
who loves you, and whom you love.

The 'West Indies' sounds such a long
way off, yet nowhere is really far now,
for the old days of slow sailing-ships are
over.

My Uncle John spent a little time at
Antigua once, and went over to St
Kitts, where you are to be stationed. He
spoke much in praise of it, and said the
natives were an extremely kindly people.

Your French will stand you in good
stead there.

Is it possible that you can come to
me for a few weeks before your mar-

riage? I should like to think we had one more good time together before you go.

You have never seen Teddy either. He is such a dear little fellow, and begins to chatter baby-fashion. He is a great pet of his father's.

Our garden is gay with spring flowers, and everything is looking delightful.

Do make up your mind and come at once. It will be a joy to me to have one of our old chats.

With much love,
Your old friend,
ELIZA.

Reply to same

Balsam Heath,
9th May 18—

My dear Eliza,

Nothing could give me more pleasure than to spend a few days in your pleasant home.

I only hope that I shall prove as good a wife and as clever a housekeeper as you are.

But at St Kitts everything will be so different from what I have been accustomed to, that I fear I shall have all to learn.

Would Wednesday next suit you? If so, I would leave by the 10.30 express, and so reach you at 5.15.

Until we meet then,
Your affectionate friend,
ANNA.

Letter of condolence on the death of a near relative

Hartover,
4th June 18—

My dear Mary,

I scarcely know how to write that I may make you feel how deeply

and entirely I sympathise with you in your sad bereavement.

But if you remember how I myself have trodden this dark path before you, I think you will know that I, at least, understand something of the awful desolation you are now experiencing.

Above all, my dear friend, do not sit and think. Keep yourself constantly employed—no matter with what, if only you keep doing something.

Tire yourself out with work in the day, so that when night comes, sleep may come too. I shall see you as soon as possible.

In the meantime,

Believe me in heartfelt sympathy,

Your loving friend,

ADA.

Another

Worthing,
24th Sept. 18—

So, my dear Anna, the end has come at last, and you are left without the one being who was all to you.

No words of mine can avail to help you, for these dark paths are always trodden alone, yet I would say that I, at least, share your grief, and were it possible would remove your heavy burthen to my own shoulders.

Will you not come and stay with me for a little time? You should have perfect freedom in every way, and see no one you would not wish to see.

Change of scene may help you.

Yours in love and sympathy,

JESSIE BURNS.

**Letter of condolence
to a lady on the loss
of a near relative**

13 *Monmouth St.*,
18th Dec. 18—

Dear Mrs Harris,

Though we have known each other only a very short time, I hope you will not think I am intruding on your grief, if I send you a few lines expressive of my deep sympathy for you in the heavy trial which has shadowed your home in what should have been a time of festivity.

I was wondering if under the sad circumstances you would allow your little girls to spend the Xmas here with my children? We should be delighted to have them, and it seems a pity that the Xmas they have so eagerly looked forward to should be passed in gloomy surroundings, doesn't it?

In deep and sincere sympathy,
Yours,
Mary Abbot.

Reply to same

Eastlands,
19th Dec. 18—

Dear Mrs Jones,

Your most kind letter was very welcome, for it brought a ray of light where darkness seemed to have taken full possession of our home.

I shall be very glad to avail myself of your kind offer to have my little girls to spend Xmas with you, for as you say they would have but gloomy surroundings at home.

Again thanking you most cordially,
Believe me,
Yours very sincerely,
Sarah Harris.

Lost luggage

Manfield,
Dulwich, 20th May 18–

To the Secretary of —— ——
    Railway Company.

Sir,
        I lost a large brown portmanteau during a journey from Chester to London by the train which reached the terminus at 7.10 P.M. yesterday.

I saw the portmanteau put into the luggage van at Chester, but when the train reached London it was nowhere to be found.

I spoke to the station-master, but think it advisable to write to headquarters.

The portmanteau contains expensive articles of dress worth £——, the amount I shall claim from the Company should my property be finally not forthcoming.—I am, Sir,

Yours obediently,
ETHEL NEWCOMBE.

To a publishing firm

12 South Row,
Brighton, 1st May 18–

To —— ——.

Gentlemen,
        I have just completed a society novel of about —— words. I venture to offer it to you with a view to publication.

I send with it a 'scenario' which may save your readers trouble.

This is my first attempt in serious fiction, though I have for some years contributed short stories to various magazines.

Hoping you will let me hear from you at your earliest convenience,

I am, Gentlemen,
Yours truly,
ANNIE HOLMES.

Letter to a doctor.

Myrtle Grove,
12th Nov. 18—

Dear Dr B——,

My little boy seems very unwell. Yesterday he seemed languid and complained of headache. During the night he was sick, and this morning is flushed and feverish.

Would you kindly come round and see him as soon as possible?

Yours sincerely,
MARY BALES.

Letter asking for friend's portrait

Milford,
4th Dec. 18—

Dear Mrs Willis,

I am on the eve of departure for America, where I shall remain for two years looking after my brother's house until his marriage, so I want to take out portraits of all my friends to give a 'home' look to my new surroundings.

Will you let me have yours?

Thanking you in advance,

I am,

Your sincere friend,
EMMA ROSS.

To a clergyman asking for a recommendation

Tunbridge,
3rd May 18—

Reverend and Dear Sir,

During the time I was a mistress in your schools, you were good enough to say you thought well of my teaching and discipline.

I am now offering myself as a candidate for the headmistress-ship of Haworth School.

If you could say anything on my behalf, I should esteem it a great kindness.

> I am,
>> Reverend Sir,
>>> Yours obediently,
>>>> ANNE MORRIS.

Reply to a clergyman who has given a testimonial

Reverend and Dear Sir,

As I was successful in obtaining the post for which I was a candidate, and as I feel sure my success was mainly due to your kind influence on my behalf, I now write to thank you most sincerely, and to assure you that the high opinion you were so good as to express of my character shall act as a stimulus in my efforts to deserve it.

> Believe me,
>> Reverend Sir,
>>> Yours gratefully,
>>>> ANNE MORRIS.

To the mistress of a ladies' boarding school

Roselands,
20th Jan. 18—

Dear Madam,

Mrs Watson, whose little girls are under your care, has spoken so highly of your school, that I am disposed to place my daughter with you.

She is twelve years of age, and, I regret to say, very backward in her studies, owing to delicate health. She is, however, quick and industrious, so ought soon to recover lost ground under proper guidance.

I should like special attention paid to her music, as she shows considerable

111

talent for it. She unfortunately plays well by ear, so as a natural sequence, reads badly. It would, I think, be advisable for her to be put to read some new piece which she has never heard played, each day.

Will you kindly let me know if you are likely to have a vacancy next term?

Believe me,

Dear Madam,

Yours truly,

MADELINE G.

Answer to same

Witcombe School for Girls,
21st Jan. 18—

Dear Madam,

In reply to your letter of the 20th instant, I beg to say that we shall have a vacancy next term, and shall be pleased to undertake the care of your little daughter if you desire it.

I may say we can offer special advantages to backward pupils, as our numbers are sufficiently limited to allow of much individual teaching.

Your wishes with regard to music shall be strictly followed out. In fact, reading of music, with plenty of exercise practice, is what we have always insisted upon.

I enclose prospectus, from which you will see that our next term begins on ———— ————.

Believe me,

Dear Madam,

Yours sincerely,

HANNAH GRIEG.

Letter asking for loan of money

Albion Villa,
4th Jan. 18—

My dear Margaret,

You were so very kind as to ask me to be sure and let you know if you

could be of service to me. That was a
year ago, when I lost my husband. So
far, with much work and more economy,
I have managed to keep my little home
together. But now my youngest child is
ill with bronchitis, and I find myself quite
unable to meet this new drain upon my
slender means, and remembering your
offer of help, I write to ask you for a loan
of a few pounds for a month or two, which
I shall certainly repay at the earliest
possible moment.

Hoping all of you are in good health,
and with love to each,

Your affectionate friend,
MILLY LEDTHORPE.

Reply

North House,
Brixton, 5th Jan. 18—

Mỹ dear Milly,

I send you a £— note with the
greatest possible pleasure. Do not on
any account hurry to return it, but do
me the kindness of telling me if you
require more. We are all so grieved to
hear poor baby is ill, and hope soon to
hear better news.

With love from all to each of you,

Yours as always,
MARGARET LINTON.

**Asking for loan
of a book**
Homewood,
Clifton, 5th Feb. 18—

Dear Mr Ellis,

I am just now a prisoner with a
bad cold, and there is a book famine in
the land !

Will you come to my rescue, as so often
in the past, and lend me ' —— ' if you
possess a copy ?

With kindest regards,
Yours sincerely,
LOUISA BENT.

Letter recommending needlewoman

3 *New Square,*
Clapham, 7th July 18—

Dear Mrs Bland,

I have just come across a perfect treasure of a needlewoman, who is quite an artist in contriving new gowns out of those which fashion has left behind. You were asking me what could be done with those lovely silks of yours which are out of date.

I have taken the liberty of giving your address to the young woman, who will call on you. She is highly respectable and most painstaking, and I have been delighted with the work she has done for me.

With kind regards,
Yours as ever,
MARY MORRIS.

Reply

1 *Princes Street,*
10th July 18—

Dear Mrs Morris,

Thank you so much for sending Miss Timms to me.

She called the next day after I received your letter.

I have already put some work in her hands.

Sincerely yours,
HARRIET BLAND.

Letter asking a lady to take tickets for a concert

Hazlemere,
6th Aug. 18—

Dear Mrs M'Leod,

Would you help us by taking a few tickets for a concert we have been getting up for our organ fund ?

114

We have not sold nearly so many as we had hoped. So many people are away holiday-making.

> With kind regards,
> > Yours sincerely,
> > > LILIAN GREY.

Reply

> *Meadowlands,*
> *7th Aug.* 18—

Dear Miss Grey,

You may send me four tickets for your concert.

I hope it will be a success.

> Very truly yours,
> > MARIA M'LEOD.

Letter to a gentleman from a widow asking advice about placing her son

> *Preston Park,*
> *8th July* 18—

Dear Mr Munro,

Will you kindly give me the benefit of your advice about a career for my son?

He is now sixteen, and has matriculated at London in honours. I am now quite at a loss to know what to do with him. His desire is to enter the medical profession, but my means are too small to bear the cost, I fear.

I have heard that there are good scholarships attached to some of the London hospitals. I thought as you had placed two of your sons in the profession, you might be able to furnish me with useful information. Whether or not, I am sure, as an old friend, you will pardon me for troubling you in the matter.

> With kindest remembrances,
> > Yours faithfully,
> > > EMMA YATES.

From bride thanking friend for present

*Elm Lodge,
Wrexham, 4th June* 18—

Dear Mr Mason,

How very kind of you to send me that really beautiful dessert service!

You must be sure to be one of the first to use it when we return from Paris to settle down as a sober married couple.

With many and real thanks,
Your sincere friend,
ANNIE DRAKE.

Letter thanking bridegroom for present

*Albion House,
Milford, 3rd Jan.* 18—

Dear Mr Gibson,

Many thanks for the charming little brooch you have been so kind as to send me. I never saw one I liked so much, and every one agrees that your taste in ornaments is excellent.

Wishing you and Ettie all happiness and prosperity.

Believe me,
Dear Mr Gibson,
Yours truly,
MABEL WATTS.

Letter to subscriber to charitable institution asking for his interest in a little boy

*Westwood Vicarage,
16th Aug.* 18—

To —— ——, Esq.

Dear Sir,

I am writing to ask your kind interest in a very sad case.

Mrs ——, a gentlewoman, in delicate health, has just lost her husband through a railway accident.

She has a little son of nine years, and no means of carrying on his education whatever.

Her husband, who was a medical man, had not been in practice long enough to save anything, though he left no debts. There are no relatives on either side who could help the widow.

If you could use your influence to get little Herbert —— into the school at ——, I should esteem it a personal favour.

> Believe me,
> Dear Sir,
> Yours truly,
> ISABEL WARING.

Letter of excuse for having failed to keep an engagement *Bridgenorth,*
18th April 18—

My dear Madeline,

Just as I was starting for your house, I slipped on a step and sprained my ankle so severely that I had to be carried to a couch. Our medical attendant says I must not put my foot to the ground for a week at least.

I fear you must have been put to anxiety and inconvenience by my non-arrival, as it was too late to send you a wire when my accident occurred.

It was a great disappointment to me not to be able to come.

With many apologies, and affectionate regards,

> Yours,
> HILDA STRETTON.

Letter asking dressmaker to call

Mrs Moreland will be glad if Miss West will call between 11 and 12 on Wednesday morning, to arrange about summer costumes.

Laurel Bank, 2nd May 18—

**Letter to friend
in the Colonies
at Xmas**
3 *Carlton Terrace,*
St Merton, 1st Nov. 18—

My dear Teresa,

Here we are busy making our
Xmas puddings, and trying to keep ourselves warm by piling huge logs on the
fire.

The snow lies a foot deep here, and
icicles hang thick from the roof. We
have already had some excellent skating
on the big lake. One night we skated
by torchlight; that was the best fun of
all.

And you, I suppose, are dressed in
muslin, and making free use of your fan
under the trees in your lovely garden.
I wonder if you will keep our Xmas as
you said you would, by having Xmas
fare and a dance by moonlight on your
tennis lawn.

We shall miss you very much on Xmas
day, which you have spent with us for so
many years.

We are to have quite a house-full.
Uncles, aunts, and innumerable cousins,
and all sorts of festivities. I have not
much time, as for the next few days I
am to be at the vicarage dressing dolls
for the workhouse children.

So with love and all good wishes for
Xmas and the New Year to Will and
yourself.—Always your

Most affectionate friend,

MILICENT.

**Letter to a
lawyer making an
appointment**
1 *Princes Street,*
Worthing, 6th May 18—

To Edwin Marshall, Esq.

Dear Sir,

I shall be in town on Tuesday
and Wednesday of next week, and wish

to consult you relative to the purchase
of a house.

Will you kindly name a time at which
I may call at your chambers ?

Yours truly,

MARY WILSON.

**Letter asking to be
excused from keeping
an accepted engage-
ment**

Hendra,
30th Jan. 18—

Dear Mrs Cluny,

I am most sorry to have to ask
you to excuse me from accompanying
you to St James's Hall next Saturday.

I have received a telegram to say that
my sister will arrive from India on
Friday evening instead of the following
Monday. So I am sure you will understand that I cannot leave her on the first
day of her home-coming.

Hoping you will have an enjoyable
afternoon at the concert,

Believe me,

Regretfully yours,

LUCY LEIGHTON.

**To a lady expressing
regret at being out
when she called**

Engadine,
20th Feb. 18—

Dear Mrs Hood,

I was very disappointed on re-
turning home yesterday to find that you
had called during my absence.

I will try to make amends by coming
to see you early next week. If you are
still ' At home ' on Tuesdays I will call
then.

With kind regards,

Yours truly,

EMMA MANCE.

119

**Complaining of being
attacked by a vicious
dog**
*The Warren,
Tuesday.*

To James Rigg, Esq.

   Dear Sir,

            While walking quietly along
the Leicester Road this morning, I was
suddenly attacked by your collie dog,
which threw me down and bit my arm
and tore my dress. I wish to say that
unless you keep your dog either chained
or muzzled I shall give information to
the police.

                  Yours truly,
                     ISABEL WATSON.

**Complaining of piano
playing**

   Dear Mrs Rosewarne,

            Could you, without too much
inconvenience, have your piano moved
rom against the parlour wall, or if not,
could you manage to have it silent for
just two hours out of the twenty-four ?

   I find it impossible to do my work
which, I think you are aware, is literary,
while the practice goes on. I hope you
will see your way to help me in this
matter or I shall be compelled to remove.

                  Yours truly,
                     MAUD MAITLAND.

2 Stanley Villas, 12th May 18—

**To a neighbour asking
that children may be
kept quiet on account
of illness**
*Ash Villa,
Monday.*

   Dear Mrs Harris,

            As my boy is lying danger-
ously ill may I ask if you will kindly
have your children kept as quiet as pos-

sible. I know it is difficult to prevent little ones making a noise, but it is so vital that my son should have perfect quiet.

With kind regards,

I am,

Yours truly,

ALICE MELTON.

Reply

Redlands,
Monday.

Dear Mrs Melton,

I am so grieved to think my children should have added to your trouble, when you have more than enough already.

I have changed the nursery to the other side of the house since receiving your letter, so I don't think you will hear any more of my young folks.

Hoping your son may soon be better,

I remain,

Yours truly,

ROSA HARRIS.

Letter to neighbour in reference to the crowing of fowls

Rose Cottage,
Faversham, 14th May 18—

Dear Mrs Hilditch,

I am so sorry to have to make a complaint, but my husband and I are very bad sleepers, and as soon as we do get to sleep your fowls wake us.

Can't you do something to prevent this?

I have heard there are means of preventing fowls being such a nuisance. I trust you will see to it.

Yours truly,

MABEL YATES.

Letter to neighbour about a dog

Dear Mrs Rosslyn,

I am so sorry to trouble you with a complaint, but the constant yelping of your dog not only prevents my baby from sleeping, but it really gets on my nerves. Do you not think you can do something to keep the dog quiet?

Yours truly,

LUCY LANE.

' *Penrhyn,' Tuesday.*

Reply

Dear Mrs Lane,

As we can find no means of preventing our dog from being noisy, my husband has resolved to get rid of him, so the peace of your household (and I may add ours) will be undisturbed.

Yours truly,

AMY ROSSLYN.

' *Comber,' Tuesday.*

Letter to neighbour regarding the gossiping of servants

Dear Mrs Maitland,

Do you think we could combine in any way to prevent the waste of time on the part of our respective servants in gossiping over the garden fence? I am sure it must be as annoying to you as it is to me.

The spot chosen for these lengthy and stolen interviews is, unfortunately, out of sight of both your windows and mine, or the matter could be readily dealt with. Can you suggest anything?'

With kindest regards,

Believe me,

Yours sincerely,

MAY WILLMAN.

Laurel Bank, Monday.

Reply

Dear Mrs Willman,

I fully agree with your desire to put a stop to the gossiping of our maids. I have already dismissed two for that very thing.

If you do not object to having the fence raised to a sufficient height, we do not, and would gladly bear half the cost.

Kindest regards,

Yours sincerely,

MARY MAITLAND.

Rose Villa, Monday.

To neighbour complaining of children

Dear Mrs Mason,

I am very sorry to appear so unneighbourly as to complain of your boys, and should certainly not do so, were it not that they refuse to listen to any remonstrance on my part, treating what I say with ridicule.

They have broken no less than three of our windows within a week, and I am afraid to let my own children go into the garden on account of the stones your boys throw. They also make a regular practice of ringing our front door bell and running away.

I hope you will be able to put a stop to this annoyance, otherwise I shall be most unwillingly obliged to resort to other measures.

Believe me, I am very sorry to trouble you in this way, as apart from the behaviour of your boys, I have always found you such pleasant neighbours.

Believe me,

Sincerely yours,

ADRIENNE GILMOUR.

Baytree House, Wednesday.

Reply to same.

Dear Mrs Gilmour,

I cannot tell you how sorry I am that my boys have behaved so badly. Their father shall know of their conduct as soon as he returns home this evening, and I think I can promise you that the annoyance shall not occur again. The boys shall themselves pay for the windows they have broken, which will be a wholesome lesson, I think.

Again expressing my sorrow for what has occurred,

Believe me,

Sincerely yours,

MILDRED WILLIAMS.

Brook House, Wednesday.

**To a neighbour offering
help in sickness**

Dear Mrs Viney,

I am so grieved to hear of your illness, which only came to my knowledge this morning.

I hasten to offer any assistance in my power.

It is so unfortunate that your new nursemaid cannot come till next week. In the meantime, won't you let Rosie and Bertie stay here? My children would be charmed to have them, and, as you know, I have a nurse and a nurse-girl, so it would not be the slightest trouble to add your wee lambs to the flock.

If you are well enough to see people, I will gladly run in.

Yours affectionately,

MARY DAWSON.

The Hollies, Monday.

**To a neighbour
asking for flowers**

Dear Mrs Ferris,

Can you come to my rescue in a domestic dilemma? Don't be afraid,

124

it is nothing tragic, but my husband wires me that he is bringing some friends down with him from town this evening, and my poor garden refuses to even furnish me with my table decorations at this season, so I bethought me of your enviable supply, and resolved to trespass upon your kindness so far as to beg some flowers.

Thanking you in advance,
Believe me,
Yours sincerely,
MABEL DIXON.

Elm Cottage, 20th March 18—

Birth announcement

Elm Lodge,
13th April 18—

Dear Mrs West,

You will be delighted to hear that my sister has a beautiful boy.   He was born at 8.30 this morning, and there are great rejoicings.

Both mother and child are doing well.
With love,
Yours affectionately,
ESBA LYTTON.

**Announcement
of a death**
Park House,
Westfield, 14th April 18—

Dear Mr and Mrs Gibbs,

It will be with sorrow that you learn that our dear mother passed away this morning at daybreak.

Though her long illness ought to have prepared us for this sad event, yet it comes upon us as a severe shock.

Father is quite prostrated.

Your sorrowful friend,
NELLY BILSTON.

**Letter announcing
birth of a child**

*Merton,
1st June* 18—

My dear Friend,

You will be delighted to hear that Mabel has presented her husband with a bonny boy this morning. Naturally there is great rejoicing.

Both mother and baby are doing well.

You are the first we send the news to.

Your affectionate

LAURA.

Reply

*Rochester,
2nd June* 18—

My dear Laura,

Pray convey to your sister and her good husband my warm congratulations on the advent of their little son.

And you I congratulate on having attained to the dignity of aunt!

Kiss the little stranger for

Your affectionate friend,

ROSAMUND MARSHALL.

**Letter announcing death
of relative**

39 *Brook Street,
30th March* 18—

My dear Florrie,

The sad news I have to send will not find you unprepared.

Our poor brother passed away this morning. He died quite peacefully and for the last few hours suffered no pain. Mother is quite prostrated by the shock, although she knew the end must come soon.

The funeral will take place next Thursday.

I hope you will come as soon as possible.

Your loving sister,

ADA.

**Letter announcing
death of a friend**   *Stroud Green,
29th March* 18—

My dear Miss Rhodes,
     You will be truly grieved to
hear that our friend Mr Willis died this
morning. He seemed to get on all right
for a few days after the operation, and then
quite suddenly he died of heart-failure.

His poor wife is nearly beside herself
with grief.

        With best wishes,
          Yours truly,
           MARIAN LISTWELL.

WHAT
SHALL
I SAY?